Sunderland College

Bede/Headways Learning Centre

This book is due for return on or before the last date shown below
Please be aware that sanctions are applied for overdue items
Renew online via Moodle
Renew by phone: call 5116344

ALSO AVAILABLE IN THIS SERIES

STUDYING FIGHT CLUB

Mark Ramey

auteur

For

Cate, Sam, Mum, Nan, Izzy, Anna, both Mikes, Lynn, Polo, Morris and
Jakki.

First published 2012, reprinted 2014 by
Auteur, 24 Hartwell Crescent, Leighton Buzzard LU7 1NP
www.auteur.co.uk

Copyright © Auteur Publishing 2012

Designed and set by Nikki Hamlett at Cassels Design www.casselsdesign.co.uk

Printed and bound by Printondemand-worldwide.com

British Library Cataloguing-in-Publication Data
A catalogue record for this book is available from the British Library

ISBN 978-1-906733-55-1 paperback

Contents

'He who fights with monsters might take care lest he thereby become a monster. And if you gaze for long into an abyss, the abyss gazes also into you.'

Friedrich Nietzsche, *Beyond Good and Evil*

'One must still have chaos within oneself to give birth to a dancing star.'

Friedrich Nietzsche, *Thus Spoke Zarathustra*

Fact Sheet: *Fight Club* (Fincher, USA, 1999)

Technical specification: 139 minutes run time, 35 mm colour

Production companies: Fox 2000 Pictures and Regency Enterprise

Genre: Crime (Box Office Mojo); Drama (IMDb)

Director: David Fincher

Writers: Chuck Palahniuk (source novel); Jim Uhls (screenplay)

Starring: Brad Pitt, Edward Norton, Helena Bonham Carter

Budget: $63 million

USA opening weekend: $11, 035, 485

UK opening weekend: $1, 177, 219

Worldwide Box office: £100, 853, 753

Rating: MPPA – R certificate; BBFC – 18 certificate

Key release dates: Venice Film Festival 10 September 1999; USA 17 October 1999 (1963 screens); UK 12 November 1999 (322 screens)

Plot synopsis of *Fight Club*
SPOILER ALERT

The structure of the film roughly corresponds to three Acts.

Act 1: Meeting Jack and finding Marla: Jack is tied to a chair in an office at the top of a tower block. Tyler Durden has beaten him up and is holding a gun in his mouth. Through Jack's voice over and subsequent flashbacks we learn that he is unhappy with his lonely, materialistic and morally empty life. Depressed he cannot sleep but is refused narcotics by his doctor. In desperation he attends, as 'a faker', a variety of support groups for people with terminal or seriously debilitating conditions. There, he learns to cry and sleep. However, Marla Singer, a similarly neurotic loner and 'support group tourist' appears at one of Jack's meetings and destroys his equanimity. He is both attracted to and repelled by Marla. They begrudgingly agree to share out the support groups so they need never meet again. As they part Jack asks for, and receives, Marla's number.

Act 2: Meeting Tyler and rejecting Marla: Jack meets charismatic soap seller, Tyler Durden, on a plane. They part at the airport, Jack with Tyler's business card. Then Jack learns that his apartment has mysteriously blown up; suddenly homeless he almost calls Marla but changes his mind at the last second. He phones Tyler instead, who agrees to meet him at a bar for a drink. There, at the end of the night, Tyler asks Jack to hit him and fight club is born. They go back to Tyler's decrepit old house where Jack ends up living. Jack and Tyler become good friends and together they open up fight club's membership to other men. Tyler starts sleeping with Marla Singer and forms the cultish Project Mayhem - a small army of male disciples culled from the ranks of fight club. Tyler and Jack's relationship cools until Tyler disappears, apparently touring the USA for more converts to Project Mayhem. A Project disciple is martyred on a botched raid leading Jack to realise that Project Mayhem is out of control. He decides to chase Tyler down and confront him.

Act 3: Destroying Tyler and accepting Marla: Jack realises that he and Tyler are the same person. Marla confirms this on the phone. Jack returns home to find that the Project Mayhem army and Tyler have vanished. Jack decides to hand himself over to the police. En route he sees Marla and tells her he likes her. He puts her on a bus to safety, little realising that Project Mayhem disciples are on the bus too. Then he runs to the police but discovers that they are also Project Mayhem recruits. Barely escaping from castration at their hands, Jack runs to the building that he knows Tyler plans to blow up. Tyler beats up Jack in the car-park basement of the building and Jack disarms the bomb that Tyler had placed there. Jack is knocked unconscious and wakens, tied to a chair, on the penthouse floor of the building. He is Tyler's prisoner. Jack finds the power to defeat Tyler, especially when he realises that Marla, who has been brought to the office, is no longer safe. He kills Tyler by trying to kill himself. Hand in hand, Jack and Marla watch the explosive financial apocalypse of the world as devised by Tyler Durden.

Introduction

Studying *Fight Club* is a response to a number of issues. Firstly, *Fight Club* (Fincher, 1999) has, since 2009, been an optional examined text in the WJEC's A2 Film Studies course in the UK. There the film sits alongside such canonical heavyweights as *Modern Times* (Chaplin, 1936) and *Vertigo* (Hitchcock, 1958) and yet, perhaps unsurprisingly, *Fight Club* is the most popular studied option. The exam requires a close critical study of the text but there are no specific books tailored to the film: hence an academic need for this guide.[1]

Secondly, the film's director, David Fincher, and the key cast of Brad Pitt, Edward Norton and Helena Bonham Carter remain powerful Hollywood voices, whose work range from the mainstream to the art house. Fincher in particular is now widely regarded as a contemporary auteur with the facility to explore the zeitgeist in a stylish and substantial way: the recent critical and box office success of *The Social Network* (Fincher, 2010) and *The Girl with the Dragon Tattoo* (Fincher, 2011) is evidence of his ability to helm provocative and culturally pertinent films. This guide will then, in part, explore *Fight Club* in terms of its director and key cast. Also of interest is the film's production journey, from *Fight Club*'s beginnings as a controversial novel to its current incarnation as a cult film. That a major Hollywood studio (Fox) was largely responsible for this transformation is a commercial paradox that is also explored.

Finally, there is the need to revisit *Fight Club* in terms of its broad cultural impact and continuing relevance. Sales of the 10th anniversary DVD re-release in 2009 confirmed the film's commercial viability and Chuck Palahniuk's source novel remains a modern classic. There is still an appetite for *Fight Club* and its themes continue to feel important, especially since 9/11, the rise of the American far right, the increasing mediation and commodification of western culture and a global recession. The film's climactic apocalypse is now no longer mere metaphor. This guide's final aim is therefore to illustrate the multiple interpretations and discourses that the film gives rise to.

Fight Club still packs a powerful punch, with its perceived machismo remaining its most frequently explored aspect and indeed gender identity and post-millennial male anxiety are certainly important critical angles. However, I wish to push the analysis of the film beyond gender. My aim is to also explore *Fight Club* in terms of its attack on postmodern culture via a proper understanding of Nietzsche: a philosopher who is often negatively attributed to *Fight Club*'s philosophy. On such a reading the film presents us with a barren, alienating culture that encourages the mindless pursuit of style over substance at the expense of personal and social fulfilment. I see the film as a wake-up call. *Fight Club* is a leftfield romance with an important agenda: it is a film which asks us all to become more authentic.

Notes:

1. This book assumes familiarity with the texts — film and novel — and so 'spoilers' are present. If you have not read the book or seen the film, then do it now. That is the 'first rule' of this guide to *Fight Club*. The 'second rule' of this guide to *Fight Club* is: If you have not read the book or seen the film, **then do it now!**

Chapter 1: The Cult of *Fight Club*

Fight Club is the cinematic equivalent of one of the philosopher, Friedrich Nietzsche's, last books, *Twilight of the Idols: or how to philosophise with a hammer* (1888). The film is iconoclastic: its aim is to destroy some of our most cherished beliefs, for example the modernist idea that self-improvement is a good thing. Not according to Tyler Durden, who tells us: 'Self-improvement is masturbation ... Self-destruction is maybe the answer.'[1] To continue with the Nietzschean analogy (something many critics and fans of the film also do) Nietzsche describes himself as philosophical and cultural 'dynamite' (*Ecce Homo* 1888). *Fight Club* is no different: the nameless narrator's actions are literally and metaphorically explosive. My point is that *Fight Club* (and, for that matter, Nietzsche's philosophy) is ultimately about personal and cultural transformation. *Fight Club* is dynamite and knowing that can really help when we explore its appeal. To some (and I include myself in this category) the film is stylistically, technically and ideologically radical. It is *good* dynamite. It is the kind of explosive charge needed to clear away the debris of a failed civilisation and construct the building blocks of a new age. On the last page of the novel we find this quote: 'We're going to break up civilization so we can make something better out of the world.' (p. 208) *Fight Club* is a text we need.

On the other hand, it can also be seen as a puerile exercise in ersatz Nietzschean philosophy. On such a reading, *Fight Club* is an irresponsible, misogynistic and reactionary text. It is not a fraternal 'call-to-arms' but rather a debased and dehumanising spectacle: the *fight club* is just a gladiatorial arena for unreconstructed men who cannot adjust to the pluralism of the twenty-first century. *Fight Club* is a film for boys who want to be real men and think that means fighting each other. *Fight Club* is *Jackass* with philosophical pretensions. It is *bad* dynamite and in the wrong hands that could do real damage.

These diverse reactions to the film will be explored in more depth in Chapters 3 and 4. They illustrate the contested landscape within which we need to situate the film. *Fight Club* is a battleground discouraging ambiguity: you are either for or against it. Fans fly the flag of *Fight Club* and it is with them that we should start our exploration of the film. What is it about the film that creates such loyalty and devotion? Why is *Fight Club* a cult?

Defining a cult film

The definition of what constitutes a cult film is open to debate but in general there is agreement on some of the significant factors. The online academic film journal *Bright Lights* defines a cult film as one that meets most of the following criteria:

1. Marginality: content falls outside general cultural norms.

2. Suppression: subject to censor, ridicule, lawsuit or exclusion.

3. Economics: box-office flop on release but eventually profitable.

4. Transgression: content breaks social, moral or legal rules.

5. Cult following: generates a devoted minority audience.

6. Community: audience is or becomes a self-identified group.

7. Quotation: lines of dialogue become common language.

8. Iconography: establishes or revives cult icons.

(Bentley-Baker, 2010)

Fight Club meets most of the above criteria. For example, in terms of 'marginality' the film clearly deals with a host of aberrant characters and behaviours ranging from the mentally ill and suicidal through to vandalism and torture. The film is also clearly 'transgressive' with its illegal fight clubs and Project Mayhem's urban activism. The film had classification issues with the British Board of Film Classification (BBFC) and there was also an element of 'suppression' emerging from the Hollywood community with many in the industry regarding the film as irresponsible. Finally, in terms of 'economics' according to Dennis Lim, writing in the *New York Times* in 2009, prior to the film's Blu-ray release:

> ... *Fight Club*, which had a budget of more than $60 million, bombed at the box office, earning $37 million during its North American run. But the film's potent afterlife is proof that, as Mr. [Edward] Norton put it, 'you can't always rate the value of a piece of art through the short turnaround ways that we tend to assess things'. Not only has *Fight Club* performed exceptionally well on DVD — it has sold more than six million

copies on DVD and video, and is now being issued in a 10th anniversary Blu-ray edition — but it has also become a kind of cultural mother lode. (Lim, 2009)

The film, then, has an afterlife and a powerful cultural resonance and it is from there that we get the subsequent factors that suggest cult status on the *Bright Lights* taxonomy: 'cult following, community, iconography and quotation.'

An excellent resource for assessing the impact of a film in terms of its fans is IMDb, the Internet Movie Database. There the fans of *Fight Club* still evoke a strong sense of community and shared experience. At the time of writing (December 2011) *Fight Club* is currently number 13 in IMDb's all-time favourite films list, sitting just behind such blockbuster film phenomena as *The Godfather* (Coppola, 1972), *The Dark Knight* (Nolan, 2008) and *Star Wars* (Lucas, 1977). It is also the fifth most voted-for film, garnering over 503,147 votes (as of 3/12/11). In the forums, fans leave such messages as: '… this movie changed my life. Not just on a personal level … but also as a movie-watcher. I view movies differently after seeing this movie, because it broke down doors' (IMDb forum: K.R., 2003). Another fan writes: 'My main interest in the film is that it does not present characters for us to think about but rather, it presents actions for us to think about. … This film is not about violence. It is about choices. It is about activity. It is about lethargy. It is about waking up and realising that at some point in the past we've gone to the toilet and thrown up our dreams without even realising that society has stuck its fingers down our throat' (IMDb forum: L., 1999). Clearly, this film can energise a passionate fan response and help to forge a sense of 'community'.

To make use of another taxonomy, the excellent website *Cultographies* defines cult audiences and films in the following terms:

> Highly committed and rebellious in their appreciation, cult audiences are frequently at odds with cultural conventions – they prefer strange topics and allegorical themes that rub against cultural sensitivities and resist dominant politics. Cult films transgress common notions of good and bad taste, and they challenge genre conventions and coherent storytelling. Among the techniques cult films use are intertextual references, gore, loose ends in the storyline, or the creation of nostalgia. … In spite of often-limited accessibility, they

have a continuous market value and a long-lasting public presence. (Cultographies.com)

Once again, *Fight Club* would appear to fulfil all these preconditions. For example, *Fight Club* is full of 'intertextual references', especially ones to do with advertising, branding and TV. It has its fair share of 'gore' and the visceral fight club beatings can be intense. It is also an unusual film that 'challenges genre expectations': IMDb tags it as a 'drama' and in 2003 Fox re-released it in an 'action' genre box set, called 'The Action Pack' along with such films as *Transporter* (Leterrier and Luen, 2002) and *Big Trouble in Little China* (Carpenter, 1986). In terms of narrative and the device of 'a loose end in the storyline', the film famously ends on a cliff-hanger (the book does not) and the general drive of the narrative is elliptical and chaotic. The famous Tyler/Jack twist is also an aspect of the narrative that gives it cultish appeal, as does the attack on 'coherent storytelling'. The most obvious examples of this occur when Tyler and Jack 'break the fourth wall' through direct audience address; the insertion of pornographic material that tells us 'Tyler has been here, too'; and when one of Tyler's powerful tirades, directed at the audience, literally warps the film in the projector.

Finally, in terms of the last criterion, 'long-lasting public presence', there is clearly a sense that *Fight Club*, as I mentioned earlier, has an after-life. The film still makes money. As long as the world the film depicts remains familiar, then *Fight Club* will have an audience and cult status.

The Cult is Born: the Novel

Fight Club began in 1996 as a short story by a little-known American writer, Chuck Palahniuk. Its seven pages now form Chapter 6 of the novel. It was first published in a short-story anthology, *The Pursuit of Happiness*. Chapter 6 is where the mercurial character, Tyler Durden, famously proclaims the eight rules of fight club. More than any other phrasing in the film, the first two rules and their emphatic delivery, struck a nerve within popular culture and remain eminently quotable.

'The first rule about fight club is you don't talk about fight club.
The second rule about fight club is you don't talk about fight club.'
(Palahniuk, 2006: p 48)

The notion of a 'secretive, bare-knuckle fighting club for men' gave the novel its stereotypical appeal but the fighting was always a metaphor. Fans of physical violence may well be disappointed with a film that has only one death (the novel has three) and where fighting is used as a means to re-engage with life rather than end it. The only actual death in the film is that of Robert 'Bob' Poulson's, whose pointless and foolish martyrdom at the hand of a policeman is graphically illustrated. *Fight Club* may well glamorise fighting but that's not where the film's real danger lies. As a contrast, the seven iconic movie musclemen cast in the $80 million budget, action movie, *The Expendables* (Stallone, 2010), have between them, notched up 2,149 on-screen kills in 32 films. Dolph Lundgren tops the field with 632 kills, followed closely by body building-icons Arnold Schwarzenegger (513 kills) and Sylvester Stallone (334 kills). *The Expendables* film itself destroys 180 human beings (Statistical Source: Gary Phillips, 2010).

The high death toll in standard Hollywood action fare such as this is therefore an indication that whatever nerve *Fight Club* subversively attacks it is unlikely to belong to a pacifist. The film itself starts famously in the fear centre of the narrator's brain and fear is perhaps the main negative energy that the film evokes in the unsympathetic viewer. However, one could argue (as indeed do Fincher and Palahniuk) that the narrative is primarily about love and maturation rather than infantilised rage. As Palahniuk states, in the Afterword written for the 2006 edition of the novel: 'The fighting wasn't the important part of the story. What I needed were the rules.' (Palahniuk, 2006). The naïve, almost childlike quality of the rules and the secretive nature of the club gave Palahniuk a literary device from which to hang his minimalist prose but the fighting was always of secondary importance. It is for this reason that successful feminine spoofs of the film like the *Suicide Girls'* photo-shoot tribute and the viral trailer, *Jane Austen's Fight Club* work so well; if the film were just about men fighting then it might have been called *The Expendables*. Its subversive character therefore ensures a broader audience than one focussed solely on its machismo and gender-specific appeal.

An early champion of Palahniuk was New York based Fox film executive, Raymond Bongiovanni, who sadly died before the film was made but who could seemingly still pitch from beyond the grave. Palahniuk describes how his agent telephoned him after the producer's funeral: 'He said,

'Your name was mentioned eight times during the eulogy. You can't buy better press than that' (Swallow, 2004, p.118). In acknowledgement of Bongiovanni's efforts, the film carries a credit dedication. Laura Ziskin, then President of Production at Fox2000 Pictures, and another key figure in the film's production, notes:

> Raymond Bongiovanni called me one morning and said he had been up all night reading this book by a first-time novelist that he thought I should take a look at. He was very excited about it, not sure it was a movie, but sure he had read the work of an exciting new voice. (DVD booklet, 2006)

This is all before the novel's publication where, '...in an industry hungry for ideas, the book had been quietly slipped by its publisher into the sights of Fox's creative fire-watchers ...' (Swallow, 2004, p.118). The book had this effect on people. Brad Pitt and Edward Norton were both brought on board after swiftly reading the manuscript and being impressed. Fincher comments: 'The strongest thing this film has going for it is Chuck's [Palahniuk] voice' (Director's commentary, 10th anniversary Blu-ray release).

Given that Fincher is correct and Palahniuk's voice is the driving force behind the novel and the film then we are justified in taking a closer look at the novel, as clearly it is from the novel that the film derives much of its energy.[2]

Palahniuk states that 'The goal all along was to write a novel based on being with people and listening to them. That's why so much of *Fight Club* was written in public, at parties, at bars, at the gym, at work' (DVD booklet, 2006).

Clearly, this novel was intended to talk to people and engage them in observations and emotions they would recognise. But who are these 'people'? Palahniuk's target audience was, at one level, the disillusioned, white, working men as represented by the narrative's key protagonist. The first-person narrator of the film and novel is never named, although he does obliquely refer to himself as Joe (novel) and Jack (film). From here on we will talk of Jack. On a wider level, the novel communicates to everyman and everywoman, to every Jack and every Jill. Even the city Jack lives in is never mentioned and the American iconography could as easily be substituted by any other Westernised urban centre. The key appeal of this novel is that audiences recognise its alienating world and the existential predicaments of those living in it.

Virtually all the principal personnel attached to the film are on record praising the novel. For example, the screenwriter, Jim Uhls, notes: 'I thought the novel was terrific and unique and I responded to Chuck's worldview' (DVD booklet, 2006).

Stylistically, the novel is an exercise in 'stream-of-consciousness minimalism'. Unlike James Joyce's stream-of-consciousness epic, *Ulysses*, *Fight Club* is fairly short, at just under 200 pages and broken down into 30 chapters. Many sentences are only a word or two long and the very longest chapter lasts only 12 pages. Most of the action takes place inside urban locations (houses, hotel rooms, bars, and offices) and there are only three main characters: Tyler Durden, Jack and Marla Singer. Using a clipped, punchy, conversational style and numerous instances of the second person address 'you', the book talks literally and metaphorically to the reader: a reader who, like the unnamed narrator, is positioned on the social fringes. As Palahniuk notes:

> People ask me why I write about characters who seem to live on the margins of society, and my answer is always that the fringe is the future. Outside the mainstream, people are engaged in constant small experiments, testing new social models, new hierarchies, new personal identities. The most successful of those experiments – what begin as cults, fads, crazes, or manias – the ones that serve people best grow to become the next mainstream. The fringe is the future.' (Palahniuk, in Schuchardt, 2008, p.9)

A style that uses the first person (I) and second person (you) engages the reader and viewer in a more direct way than the god-like third person (he/she/it). It is no surprise then, that screenwriter Jim Uhls and Fincher elected to preserve the first-person confessional character of the novel. Fincher's response to an early draft of the script that had eliminated the voiceover is interesting: 'The interior monologue is what gives you some sort of context, some sort of humour. Without the narration the story is just sad and pathetic' (Swallow, 2004, p.124).

Then we have the novel's shock value – something the film successfully maintains. The very first chapter, a succinct four pages, is literally and metaphorically explosive, including textbook descriptions of how to make a gun silencer, nitro-glycerine, plastic explosive and napalm. There is also advice on destroying 'any building in the world' (p.13). Meanwhile the narrator is unwillingly sucking on the barrel of a gun held by Tyler Durden whose 'whole murder-suicide thing' is about to culminate in his blowing up the tallest building in the world: the ultimate terrorist act and predating the events of 9/11 by five years. In a ten-minute countdown, all 191 floors will soon be crashing down onto the National Museum. And on the top floor are Tyler and Jack: spectators to the end-of-history. 'This is our world, now, our world,' Tyler says, 'and those ancient people are dead now' (p.14). The past is a failure: modernism did not achieve escape velocity. The future will be a positive place in which to live but it will be very, very different. The novel also points us, very early on, in the direction of redemption and love: 'the gun, the anarchy, the explosion is really about Marla Singer. ... Without Marla, Tyler would have nothing' (p.14).

Palahniuk's pithy minimalist style also lends itself to quotation, especially when delivered by a charismatic Tyler or through a mouthpiece of his, like Jack or a Project Mayhem disciple: 'This is your life, and it's ending one minute at a time' (Jack, p.29) or, 'It's only after you have lost everything ... that you are free to do anything' (Tyler, p.70) and lastly, 'You are not a beautiful and unique snowflake' (Space Monkey, p.134). These 'Durdenisms' were all successfully incorporated into the film and so Tyler's captivating, gnomic voice remains. So effectively was this achieved that the cult of Tyler became voguish in the real world, as Palahniuk remarks:

> ... Donatella Versace sewed razor blades into men's clothing and called it the 'fight club look'... Gucci fashion models walked the runway, shirtless with black eyes ... young men around the world took legal action to change their names to 'Tyler Durden' ... the University of Pennsylvania hosted conferences where academics dissected *Fight Club* with everything from Freud to interpretive dance ... you could walk through airports and hear bogus public address announcements paging 'Tyler Durden' ... my refrigerator was covered with photographs sent to me by strangers: grinning, bruised faces and people grappling in backyard boxing rings ... (*Fight Club*: Afterword)

Fight Club the novel clearly provides the cultish force that permeates the film adaptation and, indeed, the film's impact is the more profound for this reason. Both texts have a great power as Swallow illustrates when discussing the film: '*Fight Club* is a virus. It is not a film you can just *watch*; it is a contagious set of ideas sheathed in blacker-than-black comedy, a set of extremes that you will love or you will hate. And either way, it will make you feel something.' (2004, pp.143–144)

So you will either love *Fight Club* or hate it and if you love it then eBay and Amazon are awash with merchandising for you. As already noted, there is a Palahniuk website called *The Cult*. There are spoofs and parodies of *Fight Club*. There are real fight clubs. There is controversy. The film can still shake the cultural cage and energise deep philosophical debate. And some people really need that. A closer look at the film's audience may now help us understand why.

The Audience

Fight Club's core audience is perceived as being young men. As Palahniuk notes when commenting on the appeal of his novel: '85% of all fiction is sold to middle-aged women, hardly the *Fight Club* audience...' (DVD booklet, 2006). The marketing for the movie's cinematic release, blindly conforming to generic type, was apocryphally likened to a promotional for *Rambo*. Director Fincher was unhappy with this, as was Art Linson, another *Fight Club* producer, who felt the marketing was 'one dimensional', 'ill-conceived' and mistakenly, 'only sold the titillation of young guys beating the shit out of each other without letting the audience know of the much smarter and wittier ironic purpose to [Jack's] whole journey' (Swallow, 2004, p.138).

The young male demographic is obviously one part of the audience for *Fight Club*, as the subsequent exploitation computer game of the same name illustrates. But even in the book, Tyler (via his mouthpiece, a mechanic – Palahniuk wrote much of the book while working as a truck mechanic) shows that the possible audience is much broader – generational rather than merely gendered:

> You have a class of young strong men and women, and they want to give their lives to something. ... Generations have been working in jobs they

hate, just so they can buy what they really don't need. We don't have a great war in our generation, or a great depression, but we do have a great war of the spirit. We have a great revolution against culture. The great depression is our lives. We have a spiritual depression. We have to show these men and women freedom by enslaving them, and show them courage by frightening them. (Palahniuk, 2006, p.149)

It is then both the men and women of a generation that the book targets. As Jim Uhls notes with satisfaction: 'The film turned out to be exactly what I had hoped for – a seminal statement of the times, a statement about this particular generation' (DVD booklet). Swallow also notes that, 'Jack's wasted life, his emasculated nowhere existence, speaks to an entire generation, and not just men' (2004, p.44). So who is this generation?

Edward Norton perhaps provides the greatest insights on this issue. Speaking at a Yale University meeting in 1999 to discuss *Fight Club*, he said:

I've looked for things as an actor and director that I thought were specifically kind of generational nerve pieces or pieces that I thought were about my generation and its particular dysfunctions and relationships with the culture. And I haven't run into very many. I never felt like the films that were getting made that were targeted at us, sort of the '*Reality Bites*' version of us as a generation, were very on target. I always thought they were very much baby-boomer concoctions and somewhat over simplistic. And I thought, a somewhat disdainful reduction of us to this kind of Generation-X, slacker, aimless, low energy, [depicting] an angst-ridden kind of banal realism and I just didn't buy it and I certainly didn't respond to it. It didn't seem to me to speak to some of the deeper things that I was feeling. (www.edward-norton.org 1999)

Norton is clearly a passionate and articulate man (a Yale alumni himself) and his interviews are always erudite and lucid. (There are numerous interviews included on the DVD extras and archived on-line.) Perhaps a more objective comment comes from the critic Andrew Johnston in New York's *Time Out*: 'this is the first truly meaningful movie about ... the Generation-X experience ...' (DVD booklet). But what is this 'Generation-X experience' and who are the 'baby-boomers'?

'Baby-boomers' vs. 'Generation X'

The sociological notion of 'generations' is complex. For example, we can distinguish 'familial' from 'cultural' generations. A familial generation is the average difference between the birth of different generations within a family: in essence reproduction cycles. Indeed, according to the UK Government's national statistics: 'The average (mean) age for giving birth in the UK continued to rise, from 29.3 in 2008 to 29.4 in 2009' (www. statistics.gov.uk. June 2010). On this evidence then we can talk of familial generations as, in the UK at least, moving on more or less every 29 years. In *Fight Club*, 29-year-old Jack is perfectly placed to give birth to a new generation. Assuming for the sake of ease that most baby-boomers were born in the mid-to-late 1940s then they would give birth to the next generation, Generation X, in the mid-to-late 1960s. Of course broad sociological groupings like this can be debunked as over-generalisations but they are at least suggestive of certain trends and ideological positions. *Fight Club*'s principals are all sixties babies, progeny of their baby-boomer parents: Palahniuk and Fincher were born in 1962; Pitt, 1963; Bonham Carter, 1966; and Norton, 1969.

Cultural generations are generally defined as a group of contemporaries, born at approximately the same time, sharing interests and attitudes. So what are the defining 'interests and attitudes' of the various 'generations' mentioned by Norton and in particular the baby-boomers and his generation, Generation X?

The baby-boomers emerged from a period of global catastrophe, the Second World War (1939–45), which was of course something that had dramatically shaped their parents lives. The values that had existed before and during the Second World War were less relevant post-war and so a perceptible generation gap emerged between the baby-boomers and their parents (sometimes referred to as 'veterans'), which led to conflict. David Fincher refers to this generational conflict in terms of two post-war film classics: *Rebel without a Cause* (Ray, 1955) and *The Graduate*, (Nichols, 1967). *The Graduate*, in particular, acted as a template for the film adaptation of *Fight Club*. According to Fincher:

> *Fight Club* seemed kind of like *The Graduate*, a seminal coming-of-age film for people who are coming-of-age in their 30s instead of their late teens or early 20s [like 20-year-old Ben, in *The Graduate*].

In our society, kids are much more sophisticated at an earlier age and much less emotionally capable at a latter age. ... [Fight Club] is really about the process of maturing. ... The Graduate is a good parallel. It was talking about that moment in time when you have this world of possibilities, all these expectations, and you don't know who it is you're supposed to be. And you chose this one path, Mrs. Robinson [a 36-year-old married seductress], and it turns out to be bleak, but its part of your initiation, your trial by fire. And then, by choosing the wrong path, you find your way onto the right path, but you have created this mess. Fight Club is the nineties inverse of that: a guy who does not have a world of possibilities in front of him, he has no possibilities; he simply cannot imagine a way to change his life. (From an interview with Gavin Smith, Film Comment, Volume 35, No 5, pp.59–60, September 1999)

Edward Norton supports Fincher:

My grandfather was very uncomfortable with The Graduate. He thought it was negative and inappropriate. But my father loved it, thought it was a great metaphoric black comedy that dealt with his generation's feeling of disjointedness, and that's exactly what Fight Club is. My character is sort of like Ben, and Brad's character is like a postmodern Mrs. Robinson. (Swallow, 2004, p.120)

What is striking here is that the male baby-boomers, as symbolised by Ben in The Graduate, are depicted as confused but wholesome young men looking forward to 'a world of opportunities'. Ben's romantic entanglements and his eventual rejection of the previous generation's values are representative of his emerging maturity. In order to be a fully realised individual he has had to reject the past and literally run off into an optimistic future. Jack, on the other hand, is more complicated. For Jack, the baby-boomers have sold-out, as has every preceding generation. It is for this reason that, in the novel, Tyler aims to blow up the National Museum: the past has drained him of a future. One of Fight Club's producers, Ross Grayson-Bell (born in the early sixties) notes:

Like The Graduate two decades before, the book spoke to the frustrations of ordinary guys trying to make sense of the sorry world previous generations were so smugly handing over to us like so much skid-marked underwear (DVD booklet 2006).

So what gave the baby-boomers their optimism and sense of purpose? This partly arose from their sense of timeliness: they had arrived and they would change the world, helping it to become a better place. The baby-boomers had a well-developed and theorised counter-culture and they had something against which to direct their youthful energies: Vietnam, Cold War politics, man-made ecological collapse, prejudice and inequality. It is no surprise that during the time of the baby-boomers the Civil Rights movement, Gay Rights activism, Marxist politics, the Green and Animal Rights movements and Women's Liberation all became hugely influential ideologies. The counter-culture had landed, but unlike that old square Neil Armstrong, it had touched down on the dark side of the moon.

The baby-boomers, then, were fundamentally optimistic, but what about Generation X? This generation has already been referred to in terms of *Fight Club*'s appeal: the film talks to Generation X. Understanding the film will then help us to understand the generation that Fincher, Palahniuk and Norton claim is theirs. But how can we do this? Let's look at Jack. Like Jack, the members of Generation X are powerless. Like Jack, they are purposeless. Like Jack, they have become obsessed with commodities, which somehow they hope will define them. Like Jack, they are all style and no substance. Like Jack, they are unhappy. Like Jack, they often come from broken, fatherless homes. Like Jack, they are struggling to find father figures in the workplace – a place they feel alienated from. Like Jack, they are doubtful of the real worth of a feminised culture of therapy. Like Jack, they have doubts about the Godless world within which they live. Like Jack, they are morbid and fatalistic. Like Jack, they are fearful of commitment and suspicious of enthusiasm. Like Jack, they cannot sleep or dream. Like Jack, they are very angry and like Jack, their anger is unfocused. Like Jack, they want rules that are theirs. And finally, like Jack, they hate themselves for all the stuff mentioned above. It is therefore unsurprising that this generation is sometimes derisively stereotyped as a 'slacker' generation: a generation of mumbling, shuffling no-hopers, a generation of apathetic stoners with skateboards and headphones playing a grungy soundtrack. But as Norton has already suggested, this is a baby-boomer simplification. The stereotype may well contain some elements that are true but what is missing is Generation X's desire for empowerment and purpose, which the film and novel so perfectly represent. The title '*Fight Club*' says it all –

it fights! Supine acquiescence is not an option.

The film is then a call to arms for a disaffected generation. In a trite way this is mirrored in a brief scene in the film where Tyler and Jack attack a new model VW, a personal target of Norton's and an example of, 'the baby-boomers repackaging their youth culture and selling it to my generation' (*Premiere*, 1999). He goes on to say:

> *Fight Club* has a generational energy ... protest energy. So much of what's been represented about my generation has been done by the baby-boomers. They dismiss us: the word slacker, the oversimplification of the Gen-X mentality as one of hesitancy or negativity. It isn't just aimlessness we feel; it's deep skepticism. It's not slackerdom; it's profound cynicism, even despair, even paralysis, in the face of an onslaught of information and technology. (cited on: www.edwardnorton.org)

Although this book is not the place to fully explore the sociology of generational study, it is useful to note that the so-called Generations Y and Z have now overtaken Generation X. Generation Y (the Millenials) and the following Generation Z (the Digital Natives) will still, I think, find *Fight Club* relevant. This may be in part due to the film's prescient character, its ground-breaking use of CGI and its ironic postmodern sensibility but also, I think, the broader themes and messages of the text still connect with the young people of an emerging generation. Perhaps Fincher was wrong when in 1999 he noted that, 'I read the book and knew that you couldn't make this movie in 2003, you had to make it before the new millennium, because a lot of things the book talked about in such a startling way would be silly today, they wouldn't have the same sort of visceral impact' (Swallow, 2004, p.119). The film is indeed a zeitgeist defining film, but the power it had in 1999 has not dissipated over the following decade: the film is not, as Fincher feared, 'silly'. It is no surprise then that Mark Browning's 2010 book on Fincher is titled 'Films that scar.' *Fight Club* remains such a film and it is for that reason that it still attracts a cult following.

Footnotes

1. Quotes are from the film, not the novel, unless specified.

2. The author and his subsequent work (12 novels, at least two film adaptations, and counting) can all be usefully explored on the excellent official website, significantly called 'The Cult' (http://chuckpalahniuk.net).

Chapter summary

Fight Club is a cult film because it is subversive, quotable, iconographic, generically challenging, about marginal characters, complex in terms of its narrative, intertextual, gory and violent; because it transgresses social laws and norms; creates a community of fans and finally, because it was an economic failure on its release.

The strong first-person voice of the source novel is intentionally preserved in Uhl's screen adaptation. The use of a second-person address, which, along with other techniques, breaks the fourth wall, further helps engage the audience in the story of everyman 'Jack'.

Fight Club continues to have a wide-ranging cultural impact and has found a profitable home on DVD and Blu-ray with its 10th anniversary re-release in 2009. It holds a high position in IMDb's 'best film' poll.

The film was mis-sold as a product for the male youth market. Instead, it is a generational film, with particular appeal to the Generation X experience, the generation sired by the 'baby-boomers'. *Fight Club*'s cinematic legacy can be traced back to baby-boomer films such as *Rebel Without a Cause* and *The Graduate*. A new generation's quest for meaning and purpose is the unifying factor.

Chapter 2: *Fight Club*'s Production and Promotion

This chapter will identify the key elements of *Fight Club*'s transition from novel to film. It will look at the package of talent assembled by the producers at Fox and will comment on some of the key decisions made by Fincher during the shoot and the edit. The chapter will conclude with observations on the marketing of the film.

The Producers

One of the most startling aspects of the film's development is that it originated at a very early stage, before the novel had even appeared in the bookstores. We have already seen how one of Fox's script developers spotted the originality of Palahniuk's work and brought it to the attention of the Head of Production at Fox 2000. Here, then, begins the paradox of the film's relationship with big business:

> The production context of *Fight Club* illustrates one of the paradoxes of Hollywood as an industry: the funding by global conglomerates of films which attack the capitalist, consumer culture of which they are part. (Benyahia et al, 2009 p.414)

We will further explore this problematic relationship in Chapter 4 but it is worth remembering that even Fincher was surprised: 'Those idiots have just green lit a $75 million dollar experimental movie' (Waxman, S. 2005). It is equally surprising that *Fight Club* would become only the second film Fincher had made with Fox since the debacle of *Alien 3* (Fincher, 1992). At the time he had been so annoyed by the studio's interference that he had famously said he would rather get cancer than work on another feature film. Even within Fox itself there were serious misgivings, according to Ross Grayson-Bell, another of the film's producers: 'the studio's internal coverage condemned the material as being "exceedingly disturbing", "volatile and dangerous" and "fit to make audiences squirm"' (DVD booklet, 2006). Bell apocryphally asserted that the studio's elite was worried, noting an unnamed executive's response: 'This is a seditious movie about blowing people up like Rupert Murdoch.' (Benyahia, et al, 2009). That some of the buildings blown up at the end of the film were CGI replicas of Fox properties is however more of an in-joke than a case of internal rebellion and actually evidence of the healthy relationship between Fox and Fincher. As he remarks in the DVD commentary: 'Kudos to Fox - they totally backed us.' In a radio interview with National Public Radio (November 2010) Bill Mechanic, Fox's CEO at the time of production, was asked about his having to defend certain movies to get them made. He replied: 'I had to fight to get [Fight Club] made. I basically had to almost resign to get [it] made.' Mechanic's keynote speech to The Independent TV and Film Production Conference in 2009 suggests a similar picture:

> Ironically, both [Fight Club and X Men] have lasted longer at Fox than I did and are now [amongst] the most valuable franchises in the history of that studio, throwing off billions of dollars of profit. But they also were the leading reasons I was shown the door. My bosses couldn't deal with the unconventional choices … because the films weren't pre-sold and thus seemed less predictable. (cited on www.raindance.org)

It is, then, something of a miracle that the film was made by a big studio. Consider the contexts again: unpublished source material from an unknown author; an obsessive director with a grudge against Fox and a radical style; subversive themes and subject matter. This reads like a perfect pitch for a low-budget indie flick, featuring at best a star cameo and certainly no special effects. However, Fox were willing to bankroll the film to the eventual tune of $63 million and give Fincher final edit. There is only one explanation for this: the people at Fox, the people that mattered, believed in the material and felt it would make money. That it did not do well on its release is another matter, but film-making is a high-risk business and there are no guarantees. That it subsequently did very well with other revenue streams showed that their instincts were right. Norton believes this: 'All the major people at the studio stood by the fact that they had made a great film' (DVD commentary). What is clear from the early part of production is that Fox felt it had an important property and so it is with them and their production partners, Regency, that we should start.

Fox

The first on-screen logo that appears at the start of Fight Club is that of 20th Century Fox, the film's distributor and main financier. Formed from a merger of film companies in 1935, Fox was brought into Rupert Murdoch's media empire, News Corporation in 1985. News Corp is now one of the largest media multinationals in the world with a business portfolio that includes (along with Fox) a significant minority shareholding in satellite broadcaster BSkyB, the global book publishers Harper Collins and the more localised but no less powerful news vehicles *The Sun* and *The Times* in the UK and *The Wall Street Journal* in the US.

In terms of the film arm of News Corp, according to its own website: 'Fox Filmed Entertainment is a global leader in movie production and distribution. 20th Century Fox Film is responsible for some of the top grossing movies of all time, including history's two most successful movies, *Avatar* and *Titanic*' (www.newscorp.com). Since Murdoch bought 20th Century Fox in 1985 there have been many structural and organisational changes within the division. In the DVD commentary, Brad Pitt name-checks Bill Mechanic as an important and supportive presence at the studio, someone who clearly believed in *Fight Club*. Mechanic was named Chairman and CEO of Fox Filmed entertainment in 1996. The company, on the back of the triumph of *Titanic* (Cameron, 1997), established Fox 2000, a mini-studio focusing on general entertainment and Fox Searchlight Pictures, which produced specialised (indie) films aimed at more sophisticated adult audiences. It is from Fox Searchlight that one would have expected *Fight Club* to emerge. However, starting (as we have already seen) with the passionate involvement of one of Fox's development producers, Ray Bongiovanni, the unpublished novel ended up on the desks of Laura Ziskin (President of Production) and Kevin McCormick (executive Vice President of Production) at Fox 2000.

The enthusiasm of Ziskin, McCormick and Mechanic for the property led to the recruitment of independent producers, Josh Donen and Ross Grayson-Bell at Atman Entertainment. McCormick notes: 'With a film like *Fight Club* you need a cheerleader. And that's what Josh and Ross became' (DVD booklet, 2006). According to Ross Grayson-Bell, it was his idea to tape a 50-minute read-through of the book, turning the interior thoughts into dialogue and giving a different structure to the plot. 'When Laura Ziskin heard the tape,' he notes, 'she knew she had a movie' (ibid.). Donen left the project early on but not before he had interested Fincher, an exciting directorial talent who had forged a positive reputation within Hollywood on the back of his first three feature films, *Alien 3*, *Se7en* (1995) and *The Game* (1997) and numerous high profile advertisements and music videos. Fincher was a precocious talent renowned for a painstaking attention to detail, a fresh point of view and an audacious employment of technique and effects. The unconventional nature of the novel and its personal appeal seemed to make Fincher a perfect choice for the film. With Fincher on board, Ziskin felt confident that the project could attract major talent: 'Fincher's involvement was a big asset. We always wanted Brad for Tyler and told his reps about it early on. Then when Edward read it and loved it we had a package that was pretty irresistible' (DVD booklet, 2006).

In terms of the producers on *Fight Club* who actually get screen credits alongside Ross Grayson-Bell there are: Cean Chaffin, a female producer and business partner of David Fincher who has production credits on all of his feature films since *Se7en*; John S. Dorsey (Associate Producer) who went on to work with Fincher on *Panic Room* (2002) and now works largely in TV; Art Linson, a very experienced producer upon whom Fincher relied to deal with the studio politics; and finally, Arnon Milchan, who was credited as Executive Producer. The Executive Producer's role is largely financial and Milchan's independent production company, New Regency Productions, are joint producers along with Fox – their logo following Fox's at the start of the film. Prior to founding Regency in 1991, Milchan's producer credits included such 1980s classics as Martin Scorsese's *King of Comedy* (1982), Sergio Leone's *Once Upon a Time in America* (1984), Terry Gilliam's *Brazil* (1985) and the international blockbuster, *Pretty Woman* (Marshall, 1990). Regency's involvement in films is diverse, from Oliver Stone's *JFK* (1991) and Michael Mann's *Heat* (1995), through to *L.A. Confidential* (Hanson, 1997) and children's films *Free Willy* (Wincer, 1993) and *Alvin and the Chipmunks* (Hill, 1997). Regency has a distribution deal with Fox who therefore handled the distribution of *Fight Club*. With such heavyweight Hollywood backing, *Fight Club* was given the green light to move towards script development, casting and crew selection. It is here that Fincher's involvement really tells, as he too had a strong belief in the property and an even stronger vision of the film.

David Fincher

David Fincher was born in 1962 in Colorado, into an unremarkable middle-class family. His father was a journalist, his mother a psychiatric nurse and he was raised, after the family moved west, in California. His parents encouraged his artistic nature, his mother nurturing his appreciation and practice of art, his father enthusing him with a love for cinema. He would often go to the cinema with his father and one particular visit to see *Butch Cassidy and the Sundance Kid* (Hill, 1969), around its release in 1969, really stuck with Fincher. Later, he saw a documentary on the making of *Butch Cassidy*, noting that, 'It had never really occurred to me before that movies weren't made in real time, that there was a real job to make a movie' (Swallow, 2004, p.12). At the age of nine he got his first film camera, a Super 8mm, shooting homages to TV shows like *The Six Million Dollar Man* with his friends in the neighborhood. In the early 1970s, George Lucas moved into the neighborhood and his immediacy further demystified the idea of film-making:

> Lucas ... was this guy I would see getting his paper in the morning in his bathrobe. ... There were no big gates and a driveway with a Bentley with smoked glass driving in; he was just the guy next door with a beard. That was very encouraging – it was like, 'You can do it'. (ibid.)

At high school Fincher found work (like Tyler Durden) as a projectionist, which exposed him to a lot of European and mainstream films of the period. After graduation Fincher rejected the idea of attending film school, favouring practice over study. However, he did help out in the early 1980s on a summer programme at the Berkeley Film Institute, where he made a contact who helped him get a job as a Production Assistant at the small animation studio, Korty Films. It was while at Korty that Fincher earned his first screen credit under 'Special Photographic Effects' for an animated feature, *Twice Upon a Time* (Korty/Swenson, 1983). An Executive Producer on that film was his old neighbour George Lucas and it was in 1981 that Fincher, through another contact, got work at Lucas's groundbreaking special effects company, Industrial Light and Magic (ILM). Fincher was at ILM for three years and received credits for 'Assistant Cameraman in the Miniature Optical Effects Unit' on *Return of the Jedi* (Marquand, 1983) and 'Matte Photography Department' for *Indiana Jones and the Temple of Doom* (Spielberg, 1984). For various artistic reasons, Fincher grew tired of his work at ILM and with a few equally disgruntled ILM friends made a commercial for the American Cancer Society, who gave them $7,000 to produce a hard-hitting advertisement featuring a baby, still in the uterus, smoking a cigarette. On the back of this controversial work Fincher was invited to LA to make music videos. At the time, MTV was just starting up and there was a growing market for music video directors. Fincher saw this route as a way into making commercials and then feature films, hoping to emulate the path of one of his film-making idols, Ridley Scott, who had used his experience making TV and film commercials as a springboard into Hollywood. Then in 1986, Fincher signed for the ad agency Nesbit Neil Lacey but found them creatively unsympathetic to his often big-budget proposals. He left in the same year and formed his own video production company with some colleagues – Propaganda Films. Here, over the next decade Fincher made music videos for some of the world's biggest acts, such as Madonna and The Rolling Stones. Fincher notes that: '[Music video] was the training ground to make features in the 1980s. In the 1960s it was film school, in the 1970s commercials' (Swallow, 2004, p.21). From the early 1990s Fincher began making big budget, well-received commercials for globally recognised companies, such as BMW and Nike. He also encountered Brad Pitt for the first time on commercials for Levis and Honda. Pitt would become one of his key collaborators, and to date has worked on three of Fincher's feature films and appeared in several of his advertisements, in particular the fascinating, self-reflexive study of the pressures of fame on Pitt himself, 'Heineken Beer Run' (2005).

As Fincher had always hoped, and still only 27 years old, Hollywood came calling with an SOS - help to save *Alien 3* from disaster after two directors (Renny Harlin and Vincent Ward) had already departed. It was to be an unhappy experience: ten script writers arguing at various stages over a script that was often being rewritten on set; a dramatic budget-squeeze due to overruns on previous Fox pictures, *Die Hard 2* (Harlin, 1990) and *The Abyss* (Cameron, 1989); and a micro-managed shoot at Pinewood UK that was nonetheless spiraling out of control. To compound matters, Sigourney Weaver had secured the highest ever fee for a female actress at the time, $4 million, and the UK filming was closed down before the script had been completely shot. After a year in the edit room, Fox decided enough was enough and released what they had, desperate to claw back some of the $63 million expense (twice the previous two *Alien* films put together). It is easy to see why Fincher found the whole experience so demoralising, let alone how personally disappointed he was with damaging a film franchise which had begun, according to him, with one of the ten most perfect films ever shot: *Alien* (Scott, 1979). Fincher did, however, earn some respect on the difficult shoot from cast and crew and learned some important lessons, ably summarised by Joel Schumacher, to whom he showed the finished movie:

> The good news is you're aiming high. The bad news is you're not able to achieve what it is you want to do. You're an over-achiever, so you're miserable. That's number one. Number two is you put yourself in a position where they [the studio] have more power than you because you care more about the movie than they do. You can never let that happen again. (Swallow, 2004, p.55)

He didn't, and with *Se7en* Fincher secured a high degree of independence from producers New Line Cinema, which ensured that his vision for the film was still intact at the final edit. With a relatively small budget of $30 million, the film would take over $316 million at the global box office, making it one of the year's big hitters, eclipsed only by Pixar's groundbreaking *Toy Story* (Lasseter, 1995) and two franchise re-launches, the James Bond film *Goldeneye* (Campbell, 1995) and *Batman Forever* (Schumacher, 1995). Working on the film was screenwriter Andrew Kevin Walker, with whom Fincher would form a strong working relationship, collaborating again on *The Game* and as an uncredited script advisor on *Fight Club*.

After the success of *Se7en*, Fincher cast producing and acting powerhouse Michael Douglas in the $50 million *The Game*. It did reasonably well commercially (after international sales and video rentals returned at least double its outlay) in a market place awash with mega blockbusters like *Men in Black* (Sonnenfeld, 1997), and *Titanic*.

Fincher would follow his two previous successes with *Fight Club* and, as we have seen, his return to Fox was in total contrast to the troubled experience of *Alien 3*. Fincher was now secure enough in himself to fight for his own vision of the film that would become *Fight Club*.

On *Fight Club* Fincher cleverly used colleagues with whom he had previously worked: Andrew Kevin Walker (script advisor – *Se7en*, *The Game*); Cean Caffin (producer – *The Game*); Jeff Cronenweth (cinematographer – his father, Jordan, was an idol of Fincher's and worked for a short time on *Alien 3*); James Haygood (editor – *The Game*);

Cliff Wenger (special effects – *The Game*); Richard 'Dr' Bailey (digital animation supervisor/producer - *The Game*); Michael Kaplan (costume designer - *Se7en*) Brad Pitt (actor – *Se7en*). Fincher also secured an ally in producer, Art Linson, who in the DVD booklet (2006) notes that: 'David is one of ... the most important of the new young directors because he is willing to take risks. If anyone can save the movie business from self-destructing into a homogenized, easy-to-digest television style, it's directors like David Fincher.' These powerful allies, coupled with positive working relationships with Fox executives, screenwriter Jim Uhls and his key cast meant that the production of *Fight Club* was largely an untroubled event.

When meeting with Laura Ziskin, President of Production at Fox 2000, Fincher was bold in his outline for the film:

> Here's the movie I'm interested in making and I'm not watering any of this shit down. She was very cool with it. We could have made a $3 million *Trainspotting* version or we could do the balls-out version where planes explode and it's just a dream and buildings explode and it's for real – and she backed it. The real act of sedition is not to do the $3 million version, it's to do the big version. (Swallow, 2004, p.121)

Fincher went on to demand total control in terms of casting, script and even budget. The mystery is why Fox were so supportive. Was it that the studio were feeling benevolent thanks to the huge revenues brought in by *Titanic*? Was it due to a sense of guilt over their mismanagement of *Alien 3*? Was it perhaps because they truly realised this was going to be a watershed film, a cultural seismograph defining the age? According to Art Linson:

> It's very simple. You've got Brad Pitt and David Fincher together for the first time since *Se7en*. The last time these guys worked together, the movie did $300 million worldwide. They're looking at the cost of this thing and thinking, 'We're not going to get killed on this thing, no matter what.' They're not thinking, 'We have to put this on screen. I was born to make this movie.' No executive thinks like that. They're looking at Fincher and Brad and thinking, 'Maybe it will be *Se7en* in a different costume.' (Swallow, 2004, p.121)

There we have in a nutshell the dramatic contradiction that allows Hollywood to call itself a 'dream factory'. Somewhere between the realism of business and the fantasy of art lies the magic of film and *Fight Club* is a good example of that strange but clearly effective relationship.

Fincher famously recruited Brad Pitt to the film very early on by flying from Los Angeles to New York, where Pitt was shooting *Meet Joe Black* (Brest, 1998). Fincher waited on his doorstep until Pitt came home in the early hours. Having read the material and being equally convinced that he was the right man for the job, Pitt returned the favour and door-stepped Fincher back in LA. This casting coup, as we have seen, is really what helped to sell the film to Fox. If Pitt was perfectly cast, then so too were Edward Norton and Helena Bonham Carter. With Jim Uhls on board to translate the novel to a screenplay, five drafts and eight months later, Fincher and Linson took Fox executives out for lunch and presented them with a ready-to-shoot script. 'We dropped this huge pile of stuff,' says Fincher:

> ... something like three Bible's worth, a huge package. I said: 'This is the movie. $67 million, here's the cast, we have this many days of shooting, this is why, these are the stages we want at Fox. We're going to start in Edward Norton's brain and pull out. We're going to blow up a plane. Give us your answer tomorrow.' They called back and said, 'Okay'. (Swallow, p.124)

In July 1998 filming began at Fox Studios and on location in Los Angeles, running for 138 days to early 1999. On set for much of that time was Edward Norton. Brad Pitt was the poster boy for the film and the narrative's most iconic character, but it is Norton we will turn to first.

Edward Norton

Edward Norton was born in 1969 in Maryland; his mother was an English teacher and his father a high-ranking lawyer. Norton attended Yale University where he majored in History, while also acting in university productions. After graduating in 1991 and moving to New York, he took to working in off-Broadway productions before making his critical breakthrough in Albee's *Fragments* with the Signature Theatre Company. He is now known for his film acting although he has also directed, written and produced films – he is behind the small production company Class 5 and in 2000 directed his first feature, a romantic comedy with Ben Stiller, *Keeping the Faith*. However it was in 1996 that Norton entered the public's consciousness via his beguiling supporting role alongside Richard Gere in the courtroom drama *Primal Fear* (Hoblin, 1996). His performance earned him a Golden Globe win and Oscar and BAFTA nominations for Best Supporting Actor. Two years later, his lead role as a reformed white-power skinhead, in the provocative film *American History X* (Kaye, 1998), earned him his second Oscar nomination, this time for Best Actor. His other notable films include *Everyone Says I Love You* (Allen, 1996), *The People Versus Larry Flynt* (Forman, 1996), *25th Hour* (Lee, 2002), *Kingdom of Heaven* (Scott, 2005), *The Illusionist* (Burger, 2006), *The Incredible Hulk* (his highest grossing movie to date) (Leterrier, 2008) and a co-starring role with Robert de Niro in *Stone* (Curran, 2010).

In terms of his acting style, Norton favours 'method' as is illustrated by his decision to put on 30 pounds of muscle for his role in *American History X*. He did not maintain his physique after production and that certainly helped to create the convincing enfeeblement of Jack in *Fight Club*, which was released only a year later. Norton's 'method' extends to his carefully guarded private life, in part because he feels an audience may confuse his celebrity image with his characterisations: 'I'm an actor and, each time out, I'm trying to convince the audience that I'm this character. Every little thing that people know about you as a person impedes your ability to achieve that kind of terrific suspension of disbelief.' (IMDb)

Norton is then, superficially, poles apart from the high-profile movie star that is Brad Pitt and that is of course part of the chemistry that makes his casting so effective. Jack's neurotic, dour and whining 'everyman' is a brilliant creation. As Fincher noted, 'He's exactly that guy. You can believe that he's over-thinking the whole situation and creating this whole problem for himself' (Swallow, 2004, p.123). Norton's performance in *American History X*, with its violent and muscular intensity, is the complete antithesis of Jack, as indeed is Tyler who is muscular, dangerous, attractive, powerful, virile, irresistible and smart. The choice of Pitt to play this deeply ironic role is, as we have already noted, a masterstroke of casting.

Fight Club key talent: (clockwise from top left) Brad Pitt, Helena Bonham Carter, Edward Norton and director David Fincher

Brad Pitt

Brad Pitt was born in 1963 in Oklahoma in a die-hard part of the Bible belt that he jokingly describes, as being so God-fearing that it was 'the belt's buckle'. His father was a manager at a truck company and his mother a school counsellor. The family later moved to Missouri, where Pitt attended the University of Missouri's School of Journalism. In 1987, two credits away from graduating with a journalism degree, he packed his bags and in his own words,

> headed for Hollywood with dreams of becoming a rock star. Instead, I wound up in a giant chicken costume, making clucking sounds, trying to lure customers into a fast-food restaurant. I got a small step up in the world with my next job as a chauffeur, driving strippers to work in a limo. (www.simplybrad.com)

Such tales of finding Hollywood's pavements strewn with dirt rather than gold are common fare but Pitt was soon finding TV work, notably in 1987 in a minor role in *Dallas*. Throughout the late 1980s Pitt found employment with further minor TV roles, small-time film opportunities and advertising engagements, in particular on a Levi's shoot where he first met Fincher. Pitt's big break was as the hunky hitchhiker in *Thelma & Louise* (Scott, 1991). His love scene with Geena Davis defined him as a sex symbol: a scene that helped seal his image of 'bad boy charisma and sexual playfulness' (www.biographychannel.com). Critically well-received and a box-office success, the film led to a string of opportunities, culminating in Pitt's first leading roles in big-budget productions, most notably *A River Runs Through It* (1992) directed by Robert Redford, himself a former Hollywood sex symbol with whom Pitt is sometimes compared. Pitt's performance in that film was widely regarded as career-making, proving that he could offer more than superficially hunky roles. Then came a starring role alongside Tom Cruise in *Interview with a Vampire* (Jordan, 1994) but Pitt's performance was poorly received. According to the *Dallas Observer* in 1994: 'Brad Pitt ... is a large part of the problem [in the film]. When directors play up his cocky, hunkish, folksy side ... he's a joy to watch. But there's nothing about him that suggests inner torment or even self-awareness ...' *Se7en* would prove that to be a misjudgment. The critics largely admired Pitt's performance and *Se7en*'s international box-office impressed with only his mainstream features, *Troy* (Petersen, 2004), and *Ocean's Eleven* (Soderbergh, 2001) topping its earnings.

Following *Se7en*, Pitt took a supporting role in Terry Gilliam's 1995 science-fiction film *Twelve Monkeys*. The movie received predominantly positive reviews, with Pitt praised in particular. Janet Maslin of the *New York Times* called *Twelve Monkeys* 'fierce and disturbing' and remarked on Pitt's 'startlingly frenzied performance'. For his work in this film he won a Golden Globe Award (for Best Supporting Actor) and received his first Oscar nomination (for Best Supporting Actor). Between 1996 and his 1999 appearance in *Fight Club*, Pitt struggled to find the right material, resulting in the following box office duds: *Sleepers* (Levinson, 1996), *The Devil's Own* (Pakula, 1997), *Seven Years in Tibet* (Annaud, 1997), and *Meet Joe Black*. *Fight Club* and Fincher came knocking at just the right time for Pitt and he prepared for the part with fighting lessons and a tough gym schedule, which produced the now famous 'shredded muscle' look. Pitt's performance was broadly praised and *Variety* remarked upon Pitt's ability to be 'cool, charismatic and more dynamically physical, perhaps than [...] his breakthrough role in *Thelma & Louise*' (Rooney, 1999).

Pitt's renown, no matter what roles he plays and what insightful interviews he gives, will always be tarnished by the facile appeal of his looks. He was Hollywood's poster boy for the 1990s and this still defines him. It is, of course, for exactly that reason that Tyler Durden is such a perfect character for Pitt to play. His choice to play Tyler was not only a brave one in terms of his career trajectory but also a dignified choice. We learn a lot about Pitt the man from Tyler the character. But that said, it is still worth noting some of the hysteria surrounding the man and his looks. For example, *People Magazine* named Pitt 'The Sexiest Man Alive' in 1995 and 2000; and *Empire Magazine*, named him one of the 25 sexiest stars in film history in 1995. But he also has power in the industry as a producer courtesy of his production company Plan B Entertainment: *Forbe*'s annual list of the 100 most powerful celebrities in 2006, 2007, and 2008, placed Pitt at No. 20, No. 5, and No. 10 respectively. In 2007 and 2009 he was listed among *Time Magazine*'s 100 most influential people in the world. The magazine in 2007, in a nod to Pitt's charitable work, credited him with using 'his star power to get people to look at places and stories which cameras don't usually catch'. It is worth bearing in mind what the same *Time* article reminds us of: 'When a man looks like Brad Pitt, we tend to underestimate him'. (Keegan, 2007).

Helena Bonham Carter

Helena Bonham Carter was born in London in 1966 and comes from a well-connected family with links to banking and diplomatic circles: her ancestry includes such notables as Herbert Asquith (Prime Minster of Britain from 1908 to 1916). Her dark, moody beauty derives in part from her mother's Spanish heritage. She was educated at independent schools in London and did well enough academically to enter Cambridge University but decided to concentrate on acting. Bonham Carter had no formal training and made her professional debut at the age of 16, in a television commercial. Her first starring film role was as Lady Jane Grey in Trevor Nunn's *Lady Jane* (1986), which received mixed reviews but clearly showcased her dramatic talent. Her breakthrough role was *In a Room With A View* (Ivory, 1985), which was filmed after *Lady Jane*, but released beforehand. These early films led to her to being typecast as a 'corset queen', and 'English rose' playing heritage characters in period films.

However, she is recorded as saying that, 'I hate this image of me as a prim Edwardian. I want to shock everyone. I should get a few ribs taken out, because I'll be in a corset for the rest of my life' (IMDb). Bonham Carter was too intelligent and talented to remain typecast for long and indeed she has recently acquired the image of a 'goth diva', in part due to her intense, melancholic beauty, her penchant for cigarettes and her interest in left-field characters. Her tragic-comic depiction of Marla Singer is evidence of such a characterisation, and since then she has continued to expand her range, appearing as villainess Bellatrix Le Strange in *Harry Potter and the Order of the Phoenix* (Yates, 2007) and the four subsequent films in the franchise. Bonham Carter also has a professional and personal relationship with the gothic fantasist, Tim Burton, appearing at the time of writing in all of his films since *Planet of the Apes* (2001). In 2009, she was named one of *The Sunday Times* newspaper's Top 10 British Actresses of all time, noting that she 'illuminated the best of modern period films with her intelligence and ethereal beauty' (January 2009). In 2012 she received Establishment recognition with a CBE.

According to Swallow (p.123) Bonham Carter was persuaded by Brad Pitt at an Oscar party to go for the role of Marla and although she had misgivings over the potential misogyny of the script, especially in the wrong hands, she decided to meet with Fincher. He convinced her that the film and the character of Marla would be treated responsibly. 'He's not just an all-out testosterone package,' she said of Fincher; 'He's got a healthy feminist streak' (Swallow, 2004, p.123). Indeed this feminist or, rather, feminine aspect of Fincher's, led Bonham Carter to base Marla's character in part on the director. Michael Kaplan, the film's costume designer, also described Marla as 'Judy Garland close to the end' (Swallow, 2004, p.124), noting that Bonham Carter would listen to Garland's records while in her trailer. Indeed, despite less screen time than her fellow co-stars, Bonham Carter's performance somehow dominates the film. The film is really all about Marla. And where Pitt's allure is pure fantasy, Marla's twisted glamour is as real as her chain-smoking and neurosis. Marla has heart, compassion and fragility and this, coupled with her brassy cynicism, really lifts the emotional timbre of the film. Palahniuk, recognising this, notes that Bonham Carter's depiction of Marla is a perfect vision of 'Audrey Hepburn on heroin' (ibid.). Clearly Bonham Carter's considerable acting range allows her to project a character that is both tragic and hilarious. Indeed evidence of her continued diversity can be found in her key films of 2010–11: in *Alice in Wonderland* (Burton, 2010) and then in *Harry Potter and the Deathly Hallows Parts 1 and 2* (Yates, 2010, 2011) she showed that she is second-to-none at playing female grotesques but then, in *The King's Speech* (Hooper, 2010), she returned to her heritage roots and provided a pitch-perfect supporting role as the queen consort of King George VI.

The Shoot and Edit

With Fincher's cast and crew in place and a strong buzz coming off the production, film started to roll. 138 days later, the principal shoot was over with only minor disagreements with the studio over relatively cosmetic details. For example, Laura Ziskin took issue with Bob's (Meat Loaf) large prosthetic nipples; and Marla's scripted line (lifted from the novel) 'I want your abortion', was deemed too edgy. The scene where Jack threatens his boss after the rules of fight club are found in the office photocopying machine was also re-edited to take account of negative test screenings, which, post-Columbine, meant the threat seemed too dark (the events at Columbine High School in April 1999 are discussed in the 'Cultural Contexts' section of Chapter 3). Quoted out-of context, the scene that made it to the final cut still reads starkly: (Jack to Boss about the discovered rules of fight club) 'The person who wrote that is dangerous – and this buttoned down Oxford-cloth psycho might just snap and then stalk from office to office with an Armalite AR10 carbine gas-powered semi-automatic weapon – pumping round after round into colleagues and co-workers.' There were also issues over Fincher being promised final cut if he stayed within budget – he didn't, and it fell to Bill Mechanic to tell him that final cut was technically no longer his. Fincher's comment is illustrative of the positive relationship he had by then forged with the studio: 'I trust you and you trust me so let's do it [make the movie]' (Swallow, 2004, p.126). Fincher was still involved in the editing, successfully arguing for the inclusion of scenes that the studio wanted to lose to reduce the film's running-time, for example the 'human self-sacrifice' scene in the car. Then there was the $800,000 CGI title sequence, which Fincher was only allowed to shoot once he had shown he was relatively on target.

In terms of script changes that deviate significantly from the source novel, the ending is perhaps the most note worthy. At the end of the novel, Marla arrives with various people from the support groups she and Jack have been members of and rescues Jack. The bombs do not go off, something that Jack attributes to the bungling amateurism of the 'space monkeys' – the dismissive nickname of Project Mayhem's recruits. Jack is then arrested and placed in the care of a psychiatric hospital, where he still receives letters from Marla and occasionally meets a black-eyed orderly who nods conspiratorially and whispers, 'We miss you Mr Durden. Everything's going according to plan. ... We look forward to getting you back' (p.208). Tyler lives on in the novel. However, Fincher and Uhls were less convinced. Fincher notes:

> I never thought the mental institution thing with Tyler worked. I always felt, and I said this to Chuck, that the book seemed to fall in love, totally in love, with Tyler Durden. It couldn't stand to let him go. I wanted people to love Tyler, but I also wanted them to be okay with his vanquishing. (Swallow, 2004, p.135)

However, this does seem to change the dynamic of the narrative significantly. In the book, Tyler's work continues via Project Mayhem's disciples, but Tyler is imprisoned and Marla only writes. In contrast, in the film Tyler is destroyed but his work is completed, the buildings housing the nation's credit histories are demolished and Marla and Jack are together, hand in hand. In the film, Tyler wins but dies. In the book, he is defeated but lives on.

Another key change from the novel to the film is the scene where Tyler meets Jack for the first time. In the novel, this involves Jack and Tyler meeting on a nudist beach when Jack is on holiday. They are alone and Jack watches fascinated while Tyler builds a sculpture in the sand. Swallow notes that, 'It is the homoerotic charge that plays across the later fight scenes made manifest' (2004, p.134). Palahniuk agrees: 'I wanted to play with that, so people would be squirming, thinking, "Oh God, am I reading a queer novel?" Then they get to the end and they think, "Oh yeah, they're not queer, they're just insane"' (ibid.). Fincher did not shirk from hinting at a homoerotic subtext, no doubt sensing it as just one more level of anarchic misinformation, but it is by no means the strongest undercurrent that flows through the film. As he notes, '[It's] more of a self-love story, which is a product of our times, than a homosexual love story' (ibid.). This is lent further credence when we consider that one of the most referenced homoerotic scenes involving Tyler and Jack is when Tyler is bathing and Jack is sitting next to him in the bathroom. The scene could be read as a candid moment between two uninhibited lovers. Pitt felt it had more of a 'male locker-room' character and the fact that it was shot as an afterthought because Fincher was less happy with an original scene shot out in the yard suggests that too much may be read into its homoerotic tensions. The significance of Palahniuk 'coming out' in 2003 is therefore of some interest but the undeniable fact that there are homoerotic elements in both the novel and the film is still often over-emphasised.

Two other final distinctions between the novel and the film are worth brief mention. Firstly, in the novel Marla refrigerates the fat extracted from her overweight mother so it can be used for collagen implants. It is this fat that Tyler and Jack first clumsily use to make soap, much to Marla's comic outrage. The scene when she discovers their deception leads to such lines as, 'My mother! You're spilling her all over you' (p.92) and 'You boiled my mother.' (p.93) The lack of further maternal references and the potential to add a further nuance to Marla's character is a shame: the idea of the body fat does not occur in the film until the raid on the medical waste facility, which is also in the book.

Secondly, in the book (as we have already noted) Tyler's target is the National Museum, not the credit card agencies, nor, in Fincher's in-joke version, the offices of Fox.

Fight Club was due to wrap in December 1998 but the change to the ending led to an opportunity for some re-shoots, for which Fox provided an extra $700,000. Observers have cited the studio's nervousness post-Columbine to release such a darkly themed film so close to the tragedy. The studio and Fincher claimed they wanted to have longer in post-production, something evidenced by Fincher shooting up to three times more film than on a conventional movie, and that the summer release schedule was already crowded. An October 1999 release date was settled on following a September premiere at the Venice Film Festival.

Marketing and Box Office

We have already identified that the marketing for the film's release was one-dimensional with the audience demographic consisting solely of young men and with the film pigeonholed as a Pitt/Norton action movie. Fincher was less than happy with this reductive strategy and planned other more creative marketing options as Swallow notes:

> Fincher attempted to take the Project Mayhem ethos into the ads for *Fight Club* by having Pitt and Norton record two seditious Public Service Announcements in character as Tyler and Jack. [As Fincher says] 'I wanted to set the stage for the idea of disseminating misinformation, and I knew there was going to be enough misinformation about this movie without any help from me'. (2004, p.138)

This Project Mayhem styled self-reflexivity is of course a feature of the film itself, what with its final unsettling image of a 'Tylerised' two-frame image of a large penis. However, in terms of the marketing at the time, it was played safe and narrow, much to the disgust of Fincher and his colleagues. Indeed, Fincher wanted to 'Tylerise' the opening Fox and Regency logos but was not allowed to do so. The subsequent DVD release, however, did show further evidence of 'Tylerisms'. The rewording of the FBI copyright warning now reads: 'Get out of your apartment. Meet a member of the opposite sex. Stop the excessive shopping and masturbation. Quit your job. Start a fight. Prove you're alive.' The on-line loading page for the 2009 DVD re-release also plays on this idea of sedition with the sound of a spray can being shaken and then sprayed against a brick wall, revealing text. A final 'Tylerism' occurs on the film menu of the Blu-ray DVD, where for a few moments we witness a fake menu for a romantic comedy called *Kissed For the First Time* (actually *Never Been Kissed* [Gosnell] another Fox release of 1999). The picture then degrades and pixellates until we are into the real film's menu, a circular pan through the decaying kitchen at Paper Street and then a match onto Jack's sterile apartment. This real menu apes the IKEA scene in the film and is something that Fincher wanted to develop in the marketing for the theatrical release and certainly used in the press packs. These are brilliant facsimiles of real consumer catalogues and introduce the film and cast in a unique and insightful way. They point at the true, radical intent of the film and it is interesting to compare these intelligent and sophisticated forms of marketing with some of the conventional TV spots, which were placed between WWF transmissions, aiming to sell, as Linson notes, 'the titillation of young guys beating the shit out of each other' (Swallow, 2004, p.138). (The DVD/Blu-ray extras showcase some of this unused and seditious marketing material.)

The premiere at Venice Film Festival was, along with the marketing campaign, also ill-conceived. Fincher wearily noted, 'That Venice screening ... I was ready to take my own life after that ... it was too serious an environment [for the film]' (Swallow, 2004, p.137). Critical opinion continued to dog the film's release (as we shall see in Chapter 3) and some reactions were extreme in their denouncement of the film's perceived thematic irresponsibility and aesthetic failure. *Fight Club*, some critics argued, played with the same dynamite as such films as *A Clockwork Orange* (Kubrick, 1971), and *Natural Born Killers* (Stone, 1994) and that, like these films, *Fight Club* could itself lead to copycat-crimes. However, the film did find some enthusiasts in the critical community and, despite a careless marketing campaign, did reasonably well at the international box office. By the end of its theatrical run it had taken over $107 internationally, and with an afterlife on DVD set to transform its status and profit margins, the film was at least a qualified success.

Chapter Summary

Fight Club is in some ways a paradoxical film: both a product and a critique of big business. Fox and Regency, two big players in Hollywood film production, put $67 million dollars into *Fight Club* because the talent package was strong. They believed the film would do well – and despite a less-than-hoped-for initial box office run, they have been proved right.

Fincher returned to Fox after the disaster of *Alien 3* buoyed by the success of *Se7en*. His relationship with the studio was good and he was able to demand and get virtually total control of the project. Emerging from the world of advertising and music videos, Fincher has now established himself as a modern-day auteur.

The Pitt-Fincher combination proved irresistible to Fox but Pitt also benefited from the film's edge and potency. His decision to act against type moved his screen persona on from homely hunk to darkly comic presence. The postmodern irony of his casting is well judged too: an apparently superficial but beautiful talent for a superficial and ugly world.

Norton uses his 'method' approach to acting to deliver an edgy and neurotic performance, light years from his muscular and commanding appearance in *American History X*. Bonham Carter creates a poignant human presence at the heart of the film and, like Pitt, acts against type to create a new star persona: the damaged Goth queen.

Fox did not know how to sell *Fight Club* and so seriously misjudged its marketing and release. Fincher's original and seditious concepts for the marketing were rejected for more conventional action-orientated fare, aimed at a male youth market. This backfired in the post-Columbine climate and failed to connect with the broader youth market, which has now found significance in the film and elevated it to cult status.

Chapter 3: *Fight Club*'s Critical Reactions and Cultural Contexts

Fox's decision to open *Fight Club* in 1,963 North American theatres spoke of some optimism, despite lukewarm feedback from audience screen tests conducted by the National Research Group. The studio predicted opening weekend takings of between $13 and $15 million so the resulting $11 million was therefore very disappointing. Despite a $20 million marketing budget, the American and Canadian audiences stayed away. The word was out on *Fight Club* and, just like at Venice, opinion had become polarised and preconceptions exposed. The film now came with some serious baggage: a sack-load of negative and sometimes hysterical critical comment. This commentary arose from various professional and amateur film-critics. However, the film also generated a more generalised cultural commentary, which regarded *Fight Club* either as a zeitgeist-defining text or a cynical and destructive exercise in male machismo. Many people probably got no further than the title. *Fight Club* was a symptom or remedy, a virus or prophecy.

If *Fight Club* is a cultural barometer against which we can measure ourselves, then we need also to understand the culture from which the film arose. This is pertinent because we can then identify cultural patterns that may project forward from the past into our own time and beyond. It is perhaps instructive in light of this to note Tyler's destruction of memory, the past: his target in the novel is the National Museum. His rejection of a past that yields no future can be read either as nihilism or idealism: bad dynamite or good dynamite, respectively. Either Tyler is an infantilised teenager, trashing civilisation because he wants a Dad, a girlfriend, fulfilment or he is a seditious rebel subverting attitudes from deep within the system – a Generation X Neo from *The Matrix* (Wachowski, 1999) pitted against a world of baby-boomer Agent Smiths. *Fight Club* can certainly frighten and unnerve: a cinematic act of terrible irresponsibility which may – intended or not – encourage young men to fight each other. Bad dynamite. But it can also inspire: a cinematic bugle call, a muster for the disaffected. Good dynamite. Either way, the film has evoked a wide spectrum of viewpoints: some argued simplistically and anecdotally, others reasoned and academically formulated. It is towards this wide array of critical positions that we now advance. But before we proceed to look at the views of the critics it is worth pausing briefly to see how we can use the broad and well-established critical ideas of 'genre' and 'narrative' to aid our appreciation of the film.

Narrative and Genre

There is, as the film-makers had hoped, a stream-of-consciousness feel to the film, which makes looking at narrative progression awkward. For example, the film is cyclical, starting with the final scene and then returning to the past as explanation and then moving even further backwards: a flashback within a flashback. Another example is of course the shock reveal that Tyler is Jack: perspectives flip, reality and fantasy overlap, and when Jack starts to remember we see scenes again, this time minus the illusion of Tyler. For a psychodrama such as this, the dominant camera set-up is necessarily objective – that is partly how we are tricked to assume that Jack and Tyler are different people. But we also witness events that shatter this objectivity, so at times we are addressed from within the film by the characters. Through this breaking of the fourth wall we learn that we are still rooted behind it – peering into Jack's brain, at his mind, from the very start of the film and powerless to stop Tyler Durden's anarchy. The film's narrative is, then, radical in its structure and a film text that the conventional structuralist theories of narrative (such as those of Propp and Todorov) may struggle to adequately describe. There is after all no return to equilibrium (Todorov) and the protagonist is his own antagonist and spends much of the film running from the very thing he is looking for (Propp).

However *Fight Club* can equally be shown to resemble a conventional or 'classical narrative': a lone male protagonist fighting against a system that seeks to destroy him; his great journey from birth to death through to rebirth and redemption; a man helped by a loving woman with whom he eventually falls in love; action that solves problems and the antagonist meeting a violent end. The cast are stars, the director is a reliable name and there is a source novel. Fox identified and had confidence in the conventional elements of the film's narrative – Fincher recognised the radicalism of the novel. Between them both audiences and critics wrestled with the text's true meaning.

Fight Club is clearly, then, a complex hybrid, which resists easy categorisation. It is a postmodern text: its ambivalent generic character deriving in part from the odd combination of a big-budget studio property with a radical theme and treatment. But is *Fight Club* an 'experimental' film, as Fincher claimed? Well, not quite. *Fight Club* does not come into the art-house category and, as we have seen, Fincher did not intend it to do so. There are no ponderous longueurs or grim representations of social reality in *Fight Club*. Nor is there any evidence of a tight budget – there are plenty of costly CGI sequences and Brad Pitt stars. It is, rather, an active film, kinetic and visceral. It is dynamic and brash. It is playful, fast flowing, snappily written, engaging – and repellent. It gives us spectacle, tension and satisfying narrative resolution. It gives us youth-orientated themes explored with a technologically sophisticated and inventive technique. It is a triumphant exercise in style and substance; a slick and witty, roller coaster ride. It was MTV Fincher let loose inside a lunatic's mind. As Brad Pitt noted: 'Fincher has the A-bomb' (Swallow, 2004, p.122). In 1999 the bomb went off and we have been living with its fall-out ever since.

Conversely, *Fight Club* can be read as a sociologically revisionist text. For example, a class-based reading might link *Fight Club* with such films as *Saturday Night and Sunday Morning* (Reisz, 1960) and *Saturday Night Fever* (Badham, 1977); two films about working class men seeking fulfilment in love or dancing, rather than in their mundane, spirit-crushing jobs. Jack's rise and subsequent fall is the modern class struggle writ large. The spectre of Marx hovers over the film as he had hoped the spectre of communism hovered over Europe. *Fight Club* is the visualised fantasy of those people who read *The Anarchist's Cookbook*. It is the small guy fighting back. It is dangerous and politically troubling. That it arose from, and took a nip at, Murdoch's media empire, makes it no less problematic. Big business did well from the film. Fox eventually made $10 million after the $55 million in DVD sales and rental was factored in. Pitt himself was reportedly paid $17.5 million for his participation. If the film challenged sociological views inherent in many Hollywood genre movies it still helped make an elite richer. *Fight Club*'s revolutionary message on such a reading is not so radical despite its generic revisionism.

On another level, *Fight Club* could be interpreted as an existential fable, a metaphor for achieving personal engagement and responsibility in life. A tale of maturation: a gateway to an adult Eden. With such a reading our narrative expectations are both reversed and confirmed. The villain must die. The maiden must be saved. Order must triumph over disorder and anarchy. The baddies must be vanquished. That happens but then paradoxically, so does this: the hero dies; the maiden is captured; disorder and anarchy triumph over order; the forces of good are destroyed. These possible readings of *Fight Club*'s narrative illustrate its complex construction.

In terms of generic identifiers, the film situates itself in the milieu of the contemporary American urban drama. Typical settings and iconography of such a broad genre appear in the film as follows: late twentieth-century places of work, residence and leisure, street scenes, cars, TV, phones, planes, magazines and advertising, buses, work colleagues, travel companions and shopkeepers, skyscrapers and slums, restaurants and bars, projection booths, kitchens, basements and penthouse suites. Such contemporaneous elements often feature heavily in the crime genre. So perhaps *Fight Club* is a film 'about' crime. A personal crime is committed: the failure of self is an ethical failure. Jack is literally his own worst enemy. And a corporate crime is committed: the commercially minded purveyors of popular dreams ripping off Jack and the whole world through advertising and shallow consumerism. The film involves criminal acts, mystery, police interviews, torture and interrogation, initiations, fist fights, gunfire, explosions, the night, car crashes, muggings and assault, burns, bruises, blood and death. Add now two young, white, male, American protagonists to the mix – one of which is a world famous Hollywood star – and you have captured the key scenario from a thousand action/crime films. *Fight Club* shares in this heritage.

But then *Fight Club* is also a contemporary, metropolitan drama: a film about dialogue, a twisted romantic comedy. It is a film about relationships, not criminality. It is a Woody Allen movie on cocaine. We see domestic scenes like Jack and Marla in the kitchen. We see Tyler and Jack making love to Marla. We see Jack cry and then sleep like a baby. We see Tyler kiss and hug Jack. They drink beer together. There are conversations in the garden and the kitchen, the bedroom and the bathroom. There are rows and awkwardness and separation. Relationships are the key: 'It was all about Marla.' Romance and love triumph over brawn and fighting. Hand in hand, Marla and Jack triumphantly survey the steel, concrete and glass garden they are laying at their feet: a rubble garden from which the future will grow. Jack and Marla (Adam and Eve) are the first flowers to bloom in this Eden, sown with the dust of the past's failure. Like gods they observe the future keenly and resolutely. They are now, to some degree, forgers of their own destiny. The future will be hard won but as a paired whole, female Ying and male Yang, they are stronger. Jack no longer needs Tyler: he is able to move beyond him. Jack has destroyed the past so that he can stop blaming it and start living life. He is no longer prepared to blame his luck on having no friends, no parents, no career, no house, no kids or pets, no purpose. Jack takes responsibility at the very end by allowing himself to care for someone else. Tyler's sordid narcissism has been revealed as sham posturing. Jack is the real hero of his own life. By finding others, by finding Marla, he has found himself. And therein lies contentment. Emotional resolution – the perfect end result of any romantic drama.

Then again, *Fight Club* is a medical drama akin to *One Flew Over the Cuckoo's Nest* (Forman, 1975) or *Shutter Island* (Scorsese, 2010). It is about one man's attempt to flee the madhouse. Or is it *Psycho* (Hitchcock, 1960) for the 1990s? Instead of dressing up in his mum's clothes, as Norman Bates did in the tightly wrapped 1960s, Bates would create Tyler Durden and go on a murderous rampage. Or perhaps it is none of these but a prison movie instead, with Jack forming an escape committee on the system busting scale of *The Shawshank Redemption* (Darabont, 1994). Once free from the shackles of oppression and corruption, Jack can reveal the flaws and inadequacies of the cage. Then again, perhaps *Fight Club* is a modern, urban horror, obsessed with the night and dark interiors, with ghosts, gore and pain, with psychotic rages and profound schizophrenia. It is about demons and death: the end of the world.

So what is the genre of *Fight Club*: is it ghost story, fantasy, gore fest, medical drama, action movie, star vehicle, crime film, comedy, psycho-drama, satire, romance or fable? The answer is, of course, that *Fight Club* is all of these and it is partly because of the film's generic hybridity and narrative complexity that critical opinion is so diverse and conventional theorising so hopeless.

Let us now see what people have actually said, and still say, about *Fight Club*. The majority of these reviewers are concerned either with the film as an artwork to be judged or an entertainment to be evaluated. However, consciously or not, reviewers use different ideological criteria to form their reviews. For example, American Christians have created a successful review site, www.screenit.com, with the intention of informing users of the moral content and character of films. A closer look at how they see *Fight Club* provides an insight into their particular concerns. It also reveals key pressure points in the film that may help to explain some of the hysterical negative press that the film generated. For example in terms of 'profanity', 'blood and gore', 'guns and weapons', 'disrespectful and bad attitude', 'violence', 'imitative behaviour' and 'smoking', Screenit reviews *Fight Club* as 'extreme': its most severe category. Screenit goes on to identify (with unintentionally hilarious precision) the following profanities:

> At least 75 'f' words (9 used sexually as is the word 'humping,' 3 used with 'mother'), 19 's' words, 1 slang term for male genitals ('c*ck'), 6 slang terms for breasts ('t*ts' – but referring to a man), 5 asses (2 used with 'hole'), 2 'craps', 8 uses of 'G-damn,' 5 of 'Oh my God,' 3 of 'Oh God' and 'Jesus,' 2 of 'My God' and 1 use each of 'For Christ's sakes,' 'God' and 'Oh Christ' as exclamations. (www.screenit.com).

It is easy to patronise such a painstaking study of the film's colorful dialogue, especially if one's ideological perspective is agnostic and liberal; but what this does reveal is that the film plays on sensitivities. What is also interesting is that not only is it the far right who are afraid of *Fight Club*: it is the left wing, too. For every far right radical who sees his or her beliefs reflected or demeaned in this film, there is a liberal equally outraged. *Fight Club* managed to offend both ends of the political spectrum as we shall see below.

We will, however, begin our exploration of the film's critical responses with the 'scaremongers', not because they were so many, but because they were the most vociferous. It was their hysteria that was heard above the less hyperbolic and more balanced responses.

Critical Responses

One of the most virulent, high profile attacks on *Fight Club* came from the late Alexander Walker (1930–2003), the long-established film critic of the London newspaper, *The Evening Standard*. It is quoted below at some length (I have highlighted in bold key phrases).

> My verdict on *Fight Club* is already in: **it is an inadmissible assault on personal decency and on society itself**. At its Venice Film Festival world premiere in September, it caused well-justified outrage as a movie phenomenon **well in line with the current tentative but threatening revival of Nazism**. In particular, it alarmed my Jewish film critic friends. They saw its story – correctly, I think – as a **paradigm**

of the Hitler state ... it uncritically enshrines principles that once underpinned the politics of fascism, and ultimately sent millions of Jews to the death camps. It echoes propaganda that gave licence to the brutal activities of ... the SS. **It resurrects the Fuhrer principle. It promotes pain and suffering as the virtues of the strongest. It tramples ... democratic decency underfoot**. ... [It's] **a disreputable rebranding of Nazi goods** ... once [Pitt] and Norton form a homo-erotic alliance, ... the two owners of the same psychopathy set up a secret league of fight clubs where **the maladjusted and the macho** slug it out nightly to get in touch with their diminished manhood by demonstrating how much pain they can endure. (Walker, 1999)

Elsewhere, Walker commented that the film was 'anti-capitalist, anti-society, and indeed, anti-God.' Fincher cherished Walker's remarks and discusses it on the DVD. In Swallow he is noted as saying, 'I'd go see that movie in a heartbeat' (2004, p.141).

Walker's views, then, illustrate one line of possible attack: the idea that *Fight Club* (unconsciously or not) promotes a fascist philosophy while also shamefully forgetting the Nazi atrocities committed in the Second World War. The emotive hyperbole of Walker's language is striking and inflammatory and when isolated out of context (as here) reads like a devilish litany. However, the rhetoric is anchored around the claim that the film is in some sense analogous with Nazi Germany as well as referencing the 'Jews', 'death camps', 'Nazism', and elsewhere in his review 'the Holocaust' and *Mein Kampf*.

This particular angle of attack in Walker's review will be explored later. However, it should be noted here that Fincher, Uhls and Palahniuk do not accept his interpretation. The sorry spectacle of Project Mayhem is clearly portrayed as a wrong turn. Its members are disparagingly termed 'space monkeys' and, like the followers of any dehumanising cult, they are utterly stripped of all identity. Tyler Durden's philosophy, into which they are subsequently indoctrinated, lacks coherence and does not stand up to scrutiny but, lacking the bedrock of their own convictions, the space monkeys are easy prey. Their eventual deification of Tyler – 'In Tyler we trust' – further reflects their loss of rational and spiritual values. They become the very drones they despise. Their flight into a paramilitary existence is illustrative of their denial of life. In short, they have clearly substituted one false god for another. Theirs is an inauthentic, infantilised path, as Jack notes: 'You're just kids playing.' As for the soap analogy, which so upset Walker, if anything it highlights the double standards and body-fascism of the cosmetic industry. Any demeaning of the suffering of the Jews in the Second World War is purely coincidental (if unfortunate). In fact, the Jewish Virtual Library reports: 'We don't have any evidence that the Nazis actually manufactured soap with human bodies' (www.jewishvirtuallibrary.org).

Walker's review is, however, a useful one because it reminds us that the contexts of a review are all important. Walker is rightly concerned with the 'revival of Nazism' and he had Jewish friends who had been upset by the film. He was a teenager during the Second World War and was no doubt sensitive to his generation's fear of social decline. Similarly, he feels that the film tramples on personal decency and democratic values. It is an amoral, opportunistic invitation to anarchy. Walker's language is that of generational disquiet and a reactionary cultural agenda but it is also a heartfelt response to a rise in far right ideologies.

Walker also sees *Fight Club* as a symptom of a warped film-making culture and that upsets him as much as the film itself. Elsewhere in his review he compares the film to *Crash* (1996), the controversial film by David Cronenberg, the distribution of which Walker actively campaigned against, and the public performance of which is technically still banned in the London Borough of Westminster, in part as a result of Walker's proclamations. That either film dares to exist is what angers Walker and clouds his judgment.

Another equally well-cited review, one that heaped negativity onto the film before its general release, came from the renowned American critic, Roger Ebert, writing in his column in the *Chicago-Sun Times*. Ebert starts by echoing Walker's spurious political analysis but he then goes further:

> *Fight Club* is the most frankly and **cheerfully fascist big-star movie** since *Death Wish*, **a celebration of violence ... It is macho porn** – the sex movie Hollywood has been moving toward for years, in which eroticism between the sexes is replaced by all-guy locker-room fights. Women, who have had a lifetime of practice at dealing with little-boy posturing, will instinctively see through it; men may get off on the testosterone rush. The fact that it is very well made and has a great

first act certainly clouds the issue. ... **The whole movie is about guys afraid of losing their cojones** [testicles]. ... It's at about this point [the formation of fight club] that the movie stops being smart and savage and witty, and turns to **some of the most brutal, unremitting, nonstop violence ever filmed. ... *Fight Club* is not about its ending but about its action.** ... Although sophisticates will be able to rationalize the movie as an argument against the behavior it shows, my guess is that **audiences will like the behavior but not the argument**. Certainly they'll buy tickets because they can see Pitt and Norton pounding on each other; **a lot more people will leave this movie and get in fights than will leave it discussing Tyler Durden's moral philosophy**. ... (Ebert, 1999)

In Ebert's slightly more even handed-criticism (he likes bits of the film and concedes it had the potential to be 'great') there is still the sense that it is a dangerous and irresponsible piece of film-making. Its mistake is to assume its audience is intelligent! According to Ebert, the film's juvenile philosophising, courtesy of Nietzsche, will be ignored or missed by its audience – a 'howling mob' of 'teenage boys of all ages' – an audience that will be aroused by the sight of Pitt and Norton beating each other up. This is 'macho porn', a movie about men's fear of castration, a celebration of unprovoked male violence. Ebert moves the criticism of the film on from the political fear-mongering of Walker and ushers in a more pertinent debate concerning gender. Women, he argues, will see the film as 'little-boy posturing', while men will just get the testosterone rush they seek. Men, in Ebert's analysis, unless 'sophisticates' (presumably like himself), will see the film as a proxy gym work-out, while long-suffering woman-kind will mock men's inability to grow up and move away from the playground. These issues of gender are important and will be explored more fully later. However, hopefully it is clear that Ebert's views are also clouded: firstly, by his elitist condescension towards the film's presumed target audience and, secondly, by his over-reaction to the film's treatment of violence.

These lines of attack are further expounded upon in the next review, from the *Guardian* film critic, Peter Bradshaw. Bradshaw compliments the script, acting and direction but has issue with the themes of the film:

> In its first hour or so, this picture appears to be a gloriously spiteful and well-acted satire of our **bogus contemporary 'crisis of masculinity':** self-pitying guys hugging in groups and claiming victim status –

modern consumer society having allegedly rendered the poor dears' hunter-gathering instincts obsolete. But, by the end, it has unraveled catastrophically into **a strident, shallow, pretentious bore** with a 'twist' ending that doesn't work. ...Where it all comes apart is where Tyler tries to use the fight club as the basis for a kind of anarcho-terrorist gang, subverting and blowing up the symbols of bullshit corporate America that have taken their testicles away. Tyler brands Ed Norton's arm with a 'kiss' mark in acid, laying down a ... Nietzschean riff about how it is only in pain that you can... become yourself. ... [But overall] the movie never has the balls really to take responsibility for the nihilism, rage and despair it appears to be gesturing towards. ... ***Fight Club* is a dumbed-down extremism, Extremism Lite ... Moreover, those much-lauded, much-censored fight scenes, for all their crunchy, nose-popping verité, are as free from genuine consequence as Itchy and Scratchy**.

The awful truth is that *Fight Club* jettisons its sense of humor 60 minutes in, and, so far from satirising the tiresome 'crisis of masculinity' stuff sloshing around the airwaves either side of the Atlantic, the film simply endorses it, with Tyler presented as a deeply interesting zeitgeist anti-hero. And, in the end, this just doesn't pack much of a punch. (Bradshaw, 1999)

Bradshaw, like Ebert, highlights the gender politics underpinning the film but he is clearly dismissive of, what he terms 'our bogus and tiresome contemporary crisis of masculinity'. On such a reading then, *Fight Club* is a pose that does not pay off and something of a damp firework. It has no punch, and no power to really tackle the big issues it raises – those of 'nihilism, rage and despair'. And when it does try to answer some of the big questions it appears smug, shallow, pretentious, strident and boring. The film is clearly an exercise in style. It lacks substance. It is 'Extremism Lite' – as revolutionary as a branded t-shirt of Che Guevara for the consumer clone.

Bradshaw is dismissive of the notion of 'men in crisis' but is at least aware that it is a hot topic, one that is 'sloshing around the airwaves either side of the Atlantic'. (We will explore this specific, gender-related issue in Chapter 4 as it forms the backbone of one of the most developed critical responses to *Fight Club*.) Bradshaw also smartly identifies the film as a social satire but then argues, as indeed did many commentators who disliked the film, that it loses its way as it passes beyond the first Act – effectively the point when Jack and Tyler first fight. He also raises the unhappy shadow of Nietzsche again and takes a swipe at the film's cartoonish, consequence-free violence.

Next, we examine those who came out in favor of the film: the cheerleaders rather than the gatekeepers.

Firstly, we will start with Janet Maslin who, writing in the *New York Times*, offers a more balanced riposte to the gender specific views of Alexander Walker.

> Of the two current films in which **buttoned-down businessmen rebel against middle-class notions of masculinity** ... *Fight Club* is by far the more visionary and disturbing. Where *American Beauty* hinges on the subversive allure of a rose-covered blonde cheerleader, Mr. Fincher has something a good deal tougher in mind. The director of *Se7en* and *The Game* for the first time finds subject matter audacious enough to suit **his lightning-fast visual sophistication**, and puts that style to stunningly effective use. Lurid sensationalism and computer gamesmanship left this filmmaker's earlier work looking hollow and manipulative. But the **sardonic, testosterone-fuelled science fiction of Fight Club** touches a raw nerve.
>
> In a film as strange and single-mindedly conceived as *Eyes Wide Shut* Mr. Fincher's angry, diffidently witty ideas about contemporary manhood unfold. ... [The film details] **the search for lost masculine authority, and attempts to psychoanalyse an entire society** in the process. (Maslin, 1999)

Interestingly, Maslin references other films of the period that also reflect the zeitgeist: films that play with a cultural uncertainty over gender roles, personal identities and social meaning. She also emphasises male identity in search of a 'lost masculine authority' and notes that Fincher's stylistic flourishes work with the material rather than against it. Finally, she defines *Fight Club* in terms of 'a sardonic, testosterone-fuelled science fiction' film, which would arguably place it in such system busting, dystopian company as *Brazil* (Gilliam, 1985), *Metropolis* (Lang, 1927) and *Moon* (Jones, 2009).

Our next review, written to commemorate the film's tenth anniversary, comes from *Empire*, the UK's top-selling, special-interest film magazine. It comically alludes to the media furor that accompanied the film and suggests that the ambivalent narrative is in fact one of the film's strengths:

> Surfing a boiling wave of **utterly predictable tabloid controversy**, this 'Monstrous Movie' (*Daily Mail*) [is] so devastatingly toxic that its very existence is not only responsible for every post-kebab scuffle, but the soaring divorce rate, teenage alcoholism and the terminal inadequacy of frozen pizza. ... Fincher's film is **a molasses-black comedy** shot through with his blistering, hyper-kinetic style ... and standout performances from Pitt and Norton. ...
>
> ... **[Fincher] presents a maelstrom of celluloid sorcery.** Flash cuts, subliminal images, fake cue dots, jumping film ... while the fights themselves – vicious brawls accompanied by the sound of cracking bones – herald the movie's most subversive image: men's blood-drenched, caved-in heads sporting huge, almost post-coital, smiles. But then it starts to go awry.
>
> From the moment Project Mayhem is instituted, some of the sly blackness leaks out, and after a slew of implausibilities in the last half hour – including a twist out of the bottom of a cornflakes packet – **it degenerates into an entertaining but vacuous comedy**. (Smith, 2009)

Smith's take on the film shares something with that of its detractors, who argue that the film loses its way with the formation of Project Mayhem. However, he differs significantly in his ironic response to the film's violence. In his view, the film is after all a black comedy with satirical pretensions that are ultimately not delivered. He also draws attention to the film's homoeroticism in the semi-naked fights and highlights the superb performances of Pitt and Norton. Smith finally notes the cinematic techniques that make this film challenging and subversive – Fincher's 'celluloid sorcery'.[1]

The next review, by James Berardinelli, first appeared online and raises comparisons with such controversial films as *A Clockwork Orange*: a film which created a moral panic in the 1970s to do with its supposed negative effect on young audiences. The reviewer raises the spectre of the massacre at Columbine but in terms of a symptom rather than a cause:

> With its kinetic style, visceral approach, compelling storyline, and powerful social message, *Fight Club* makes a commanding case to be considered **the 90s version of *A Clockwork Orange***. ... One could call this MTV style, but, unlike many equally frantic movies, there's a reason for each quick cut beyond preventing viewers from becoming bored. ... The satire, violence, and unpredictable narrative make **a lasting and forceful statement about modern-day society**. It's a timely message that hints at why there are post office shootings and kids in schools killing their fellow students. By blaming movies like *Fight Club* for real-life horrors, politicians want us to look at the world through rose-colored glasses that they have tinted. ... [The] **marriage of adrenaline and intelligence** will make *Fight Club* a contender for many Best 10 lists at the end of 1999. (Berardinelli, 1999)

Berardinelli notes that what the film really achieves is the 'marriage of adrenaline and intelligence'. It is an action movie for the thinking viewer, a film of generic variation and much more than a witless exercise in 'MTV style' (a familiar criticism of Fincher). Indeed, it has 'a timely message' which many people have mistakenly blamed for 'real life horrors' like Columbine. It is a film that disturbs precisely because it resists facile answers to complex problems. On this reading, *Fight Club* is an important social commentary, 'a lasting and forceful statement about modern-day society'.

Scott Mantz develops a similar line of criticism, stressing the point that the theme of a text does not by some magical association recreate itself in society. Films are all too frequently demonised as causes of social problems rather than as social commentaries intended to help understand and perhaps even resolve such problems. As Mantz suggests, *Fight Club*'s essence is to reawaken the audience to the deeper issues that lie behind outbursts of indiscriminate violence such as happened at Columbine:

> Not since Oliver Stone's *Natural Born Killers* came out in 1994 has a film been released to such intense controversy. In the aftermath of the Columbine tragedy, Hollywood has been under the gun (no pun intended) for its negative influence on society. ... Ultimately, **citing *Fight Club* as 'irresponsible film-making' for its glorification of violence is**

about as absurd as citing _American History X_ for its glorification of the skinhead movement. Don't take it so seriously. _Fight Club_ is just a movie. However, if you are going to get any messages from it, there is a positive one that's loud and clear: wake up. (Mantz, 1999)

A frequently quoted review by the leading American entertainment magazine _Variety_ illustrates the way Pitt and Bonham Carter successfully reconstructed their star images, and shows how Uhls' script humanised Fincher's perceived cold style with humorous observations on contemporary life:

Rarely has a film been so keyed into its time ... [a] bold, inventive, sustained adrenaline rush of a movie ... in debuting screenwriter Jim **Uhls' clever, savagely witty script** and the unremitting volley of information it launches, Fincher has found the perfect countermeasures to balance **his coldly atmospheric, often distancing style**. ...Uhls' stimulating screenplay explores its **existential themes** articulately and accessibly, unleashing a steady stream of humor, razor-sharp dialogue, droll popular culture references and **wry comments on consumerism, corporate culture and capitalism** ... Pitt is cool, charismatic and more dynamically physical perhaps than he has been since his breakthrough role in _Thelma and Louise_, while Bonham Carter, outfitted like a gothic prom queen and spouting acerbic maxims with attitude to burn, demolishes any residue of her buttoned-up Merchant-Ivory image in a tough, sharp-edged turn. (Rooney, 1999)

Amy Taubin, in her _Sight and Sound_ review, suggests that the film's real power derives from its radical technical nature. Taubin credits it with being part of a cinematic vanguard ushering in a new and exciting age of digitalised film-making. An age whereby an action film is really nothing to do with action in the real world but rather the world of what science fiction writer and guru, J. G. Ballard called 'inner space'.

Like the novel, the film disrupts narrative sequencing and expresses some pretty **subversive, right-on-the-zeitgeist ideas about masculinity and our name-brand, bottom-line society** – ideas you're unlikely to find so openly broadcast in any other Hollywood movie. ... **The twist subverts what for 100 years has been an essential premise of cinema – that it is an index of the physical world** – to leave it out of this analysis does the film an injustice. Especially since this premise will become part of ancient history when film is transformed from a photographic medium to a digital electronic medium – and *Fight Club* is nothing if not a glimpse of that future. ... One needs a new vocabulary to describe the vertiginous depiction of space and time in *Fight Club*. Pans and tilts and tracks just won't do. **Fight Club is an action film that's all about interiority**. (Taubin, 1999)

Censorship and Classification

Fight Club received an '18' certificate or its regional equivalent in virtually every key territory it opened in, restricting it to viewers of 18 or over, other than in the USA. There, the MPAA (Motion Picture Association of America) were most concerned about the film's sexual content but still passed it as 'R' allowing children under 17 if accompanied by an adult. The next rating category, 'NC-17', is widely considered financial death for a studio film and certainly for a studio feature. One can only imagine the backroom lobbying that got *Fight Club* passed at 'R' without massive cuts being made. However, it was in the UK, at the London-based offices of the BBFC (British Board of Film Classification) that the film met with censorship difficulties. The story is neatly detailed in a student-friendly case study section on the BBFC's website (a section called SBBFC). An edited version of it is given here.

> There was much debate about the film's subject matter – it was seen as a blackly comic satire of capitalism and consumerism; as an exploration of the loss of male identity in a feminised society, and as about violence as a way in which the powerless male can reassert himself against the corporate world he inhabits. Whatever the meaning, the film presented sequences in which men challenged other men to beat them up, and then allowed their opponents to do so without any resistance from their 'victims', the result being scenes of strong, and sometimes bloody, violence.

> The film, which came with an '18' request from its distributor, 20th Century Fox, was seen by most of the Board's examiners, and also by the BBFC Director, Robin Duval ... provoking a wide range of opinion. While BBFC examiners found the film stylish and challenging, and some felt an uncut '18' was acceptable for this adult viewing experience, there

were concerns under the existing Guidelines about the glamourisation of violence and the potential for encouraging an interest in organised bare-fist fighting. Neither the novel nor the film condoned brutal fighting, as the conclusion of the narrative makes clear.

After extensive consideration, the final decision was taken to require cuts under the Guidelines of between six and seven seconds to two scenes, both of which, it was felt, focused on the pleasures of beating the faces of helpless victims to a bloody mess. ... In practice it is difficult to detect where the cuts were made, but it was felt that the effect was successful in reducing the sense of sadistic pleasure in inflicting violence. With these cuts made, an '18' certificate was given. The Consumer Advice read 'Passed "18" for occasional strong violence'. (www.sbbfc)

Fincher claims that the cuts were actually counter-productive and possibly even intensified the fight sequences. Norton noted that it is as much the Academy Award nominated sound editing as it is the actual physical visual beating that shocks. Nevertheless, the cuts were made – controversy had led to censorship.

1999: Cultural Contexts

Finally in this chapter, we need to contextualise the period – 1999, the end of the millennium. When any significant time period ends there is often a sense of trepidation and reflection: the past is summarised and the future contemplated. The millennial changeover that culminated in global celebration at the end of 1999 was characterised by bold public projects, such as the Millennium Dome in London. These projects spoke of pride, posterity and confidence. But equally, there was anxiety at what the future might hold and what the past had actually been like. Postmodernism was now the dominant cultural theory and the old grand narratives of historical progression, scientific endeavor and the search for essentialist truths had been besmirched. The past was a home both to nostalgia and horror. A very specific aspect of this anxiety found its expression in the much-feared 'Millennium Computer Bug' scare. As the digitalised clocks all moved to zero, the computer systems of the planet would crash and the fantasy of *Fight Club* would become a grim reality as financial systems around the world went into freefall. Or not, as it turned out.

On a cultural and political level there was, then, clearly a sense of millennial anxiety but it was exacerbated by a number of important events. There was ethnic war in Europe among the old regions that had comprised Yugoslavia. This was a brutal conflict, which shook European identity to its core. To further unsettle notions of European identity, the Euro became the common currency at the start of 1999 for 14 countries, including France, Italy, Germany and Spain. The old currencies that had helped define national identities, like the German mark and the French franc were now destined to become historical oddities.

On a global level, October 12 1999 was commemorated as the symbolic moment when the human population of the planet tipped six billion (eleven years on in October 2011 the symbolic seventh billionth human has now been born). Individuality seemed dwarfed by the realisation that we now formed part of a six billion-strong human family. In terms of Generation X clashing with the baby-boomers, the violent debacle of the music festival revival in New York State, Woodstock '99, showed very clearly that slacker values and hippy values had little in common.

There was the continuing debate over gender identity and men in crisis – an old argument given new impetus by a number of events, such as the high-profile triumph of the American women's football team at the 1999 World Cup. Prior to this the 'Iron John' movement of the early 1990s, championed by the American poet Robert Bly, had led to the formation of male support groups. Towards the end of the 1990s the notion of 'males in crisis' was given further credibility by American journalist and academic Susan Faludi's best-selling study of the disenfranchised male, *Stiffed: The Betrayal of the American Man*. (There is more on Bly and Faludi in Chapter 4.) In counterpoint to the male identity crisis was the mid-1990s cultural movement that was neatly encapsulated by the Spice Girls' mantra, 'Girl Power'.

However, one event in particular has become wrapped up with *Fight Club*'s infamy: the Columbine High School massacre of April 20 1999. Twelve students and one teacher died directly at the hands of two heavily armed fellow students. Twenty-five students were also injured, some critically. Although, tragically, by no means a unique event in American history, Columbine was deeply shocking and exposed an American culture, already suffering from millennial anxiety, gender crises and generational unease, to yet more self-analysis and questioning. Against this highly charged background, Fox pushed back the release date of *Fight Club* and the critics lay in wait.

1999: Film Contexts

In terms of the Academy Awards for films released in 1999 it is no surprise to see *American Beauty* (Mendes) dominating as it did at the Golden Globes and the BAFTAS: it won Oscars for Best Picture, Best Actor and Best Director. *Fight Club*, as we have already noted, was virtually ignored. Indeed *American Beauty* is, interestingly, just one of a number of contemporaneous films that (like *Fight Club* and *The Matrix*) focused on men's inability to feel and engage with reality in a meaningful way – see also *Magnolia* (Anderson, 1999) and *Happiness* (Solondz, 1998).

The global box office figures for 1999 – reproduced below courtesy of Box Office Mojo – are also revealing. *Fight Club*, in a list of the year's 40 world-wide big hitters, comes in at 39th. It is quite clearly, and most seriously for Fox, the second lowest grossing film on the list in terms of US box office and actually the lowest-grossing film at the US box office of US origin (only Studio Ghibli's Japanese-originated *Princess Mononoke*, at number 28 on the list, earned less in the US).

Box Office Mojo: Top box office hits of 1999

Rank	Title	Studio	World	USA	Overseas
1	Star Wars: Episode I - The Phantom Menace	Fox	$924.3	$431.1	$493.2
2	The Sixth Sense	BV	$672.8	$293.5	$379.3
3	Toy Story 2	BV	$485.0	$245.9	$239.2
4	The Matrix	WB	$463.5	$171.5	$292.0
5	Tarzan	BV	$448.2	$171.1	$277.1
6	The Mummy	Uni.	$415.9	$155.4	$260.5
7	Notting Hill	Uni.	$363.9	$116.1	$247.8

Rank	Title	Studio	World	USA	Overseas
8	The World Is Not Enough	MGM	$361.8	$126.9	$234.9
9	American Beauty	DW	$356.3	$130.1	$226.2
10	Austin Powers: The Spy Who Shagged Me	NL	$312.0	$206.0	$106.0
11	Runaway Bride	Par.	$309.5	$152.3	$157.2
12	Stuart Little	Sony	$300.1	$140.0	$160.1
13	The Green Mile	WB	$286.8	$136.8	$150.0
14	The Blair Witch Project	Art.	$248.6	$140.5	$108.1
15	American Pie	Uni.	$235.5	$102.6	$132.9
16	Big Daddy	Sony	$234.8	$163.5	$71.3
17	Wild Wild West	WB	$222.1	$113.8	$108.3
18	Entrapment	Fox	$212.4	$87.7	$124.7
19	End of Days	Uni.	$212.0	$66.9	$145.1
20	Sleepy Hollow	Par.	$206.1	$101.1	$105.0
21	Double Jeopardy	Par.	$177.8	$116.7	$61.1
22	The Haunting	DW	$177.3	$91.4	$85.9
23	Analyze This	WB	$176.9	$106.9	$70.0
24	Deep Blue Sea	WB	$164.6	$73.6	$91.0
25	Pokemon: The First Movie	WB	$163.6	$85.7	$77.9
26	Eyes Wide Shut	WB	$162.1	$55.7	$106.4
27	Payback	Par.	$161.6	$81.5	$80.1
28	Princess Mononoke	Mira.	$159.4	$2.4	$157.0
29	The Bone Collector	Uni.	$151.5	$66.5	$85.0
30	The General's Daughter	Par.	$149.7	$102.7	$47.0
31	Inspector Gadget	BV	$134.4	$97.4	$37.0
32	The Talented Mr. Ripley	Par.	$128.8	$81.3	$47.5
33	The Thomas Crown Affair	MGM	$124.3	$69.3	$55.0
34	Message in a Bottle	WB	$118.9	$52.9	$66.0
35	Blue Streak	Sony	$117.8	$68.5	$49.2
36	Anna and the King	Fox	$114.0	$39.3	$74.7

Rank	Title	Studio	World	USA	Overseas
37	Three Kings	WB	$107.8	$60.7	$47.1
38	She's All That	Mira.	$103.2	$63.4	$39.8
39	**Fight Club**	**Fox**	**$100.9**	**$37.0**	**$63.8**
40	Any Given Sunday	WB	$100.2	$75.5	$24.7

Finally, a feature article published in *Entertainment Weekly* in November 1999 neatly encapsulates both the film industry's and critical community's excitement in what was regarded as a game-changing year for film. The article was titled *1999: The Year that Changed the Movies* and I quote from it below.

Entertainment weekly. 1999: The Year That Changed Movies

[1999 is] the year when a new generation of directors – weaned on cyberspace and ... Pac-Man ... snatched the flickering torch from the aging rebels of the 1970s: the year when the whole concept of 'making a movie' got turned on its head.

Skeptical? Consider the evidence: The whirling cyberdelic Xanadu of *The Matrix*. The relentless, rapid-fire overload of *Fight Club*. The muddy hyperrealism of *The Blair Witch Project*. The freak show of *Being John Malkovich*. The way time itself gets fractured and tossed around in *The Limey* and *Go* and *Run Lola Run*. The spooky necro-poetry of *American Beauty* and *The Sixth Sense*. The bratty iconoclasm of *Dogma*. The San Fernando Valley sprawl of this winter's *Magnolia*. Were you prone to theatrical pronouncements, you might say that not since the annus mirabilis of *The Wizard of Oz*, *Gone With the Wind*, and *Stagecoach* has Hollywood brought so many narrative innovations screaming into the mainstream. ... The rules that have governed the silver screen for nearly a century amount to little more than an illusion. 'Hollywood narrative film is in its death throes right now and people are looking for something else,' declares R.E.M.'s Michael Stipe, who produced *Being John Malkovich*.

...You don't 'watch' a film like *Fight Club*; you mainline a deluge of visual and sonic information (including a hefty chunk of the IKEA catalogue) straight into your cranium. The director, David Fincher, remembers telling one of his producers: 'Don't worry, the audience will be able

to follow this. This is not unspooling your tale. This is downloading.'
(Gordinier, 1999)

What makes this article so striking is that the writer is fascinated by the democratic potential offered by the new digital film-making formats. He is also clearly sounding the death knell of the baby-boomer generation of film-makers, while championing the arrival of a new group of Generation X/Y film-makers and audiences. A rapid editing style arrives courtesy of familiarity with the internet, video games and music video. There is dissatisfaction with conventional narrative film-making techniques, such as the three-act story structure, high resolution and a desire for continuity in time and space. However, more than ten years on from such pronouncements we can see that they are tinged with the fanaticism of idealism. The old guard is always eventually supplanted by the new – who then, of course, become the old guard themselves. However, in other ways the article is sharply prescient. Postmodern playfulness has persisted to infiltrate the mainstream, Tarantino is virtually beatified, and the DIY ethic of *The Blair Witch Project* (Myrick/Sanchez, 1999) has opened the gates to such 'wobblycam' cinematic events as *Cloverfield* (Abrams, 2008), *[Rec]* (Balaguero/Plaza, 2007) and *Paranormal Activity* (Peli, 2007). Fincher (and the likes of Spike Jonze, Sam Raimi, Darren Aronofsky and Christopher Nolan) may well have become the establishment, but the aesthetic and technological revolution was accurately announced in 1999. Perhaps the explosion of 3D in 2010 is the start of a new, studio-led era. CGI may have rewritten the film textbook, but the boomer generation as well as the new kids on the block have embraced it. Whatever the case, 1999's crop of film-makers continue to produce interesting work and the technologies used then have since become the norm. *Fight Club* can therefore be seen in this cinematic context: it rode a wave that is only now crashing on the shore.

Footnotes

2. For example, the use of the subliminal-Tylers, the CGI track and crane shots, the use of on screen text and the many instances of breaking the fourth wall not least the insertion of a pornographic still at the end of the film, possibly by Tyler Durden himself.

Chapter Summary

Fight Club has a complex, postmodern approach to genre and narrative, reflected in the difficulty organisations like IMDb and Fox had in categorising the film. The film hovers upon the margins of generic identification and can accordingly be read in many different ways. *Fight Club* has many identities. It is a generic hybrid that resists categorisation and a narrative that avoids precise resolution. Character development occurs, Jack and Marla go on a journey of self-discovery, but their futures remain uncertain.

Critical responses were wide ranging but the most vociferous and aggressive were from renowned critics like Roger Ebert and Alexander Walker who found the film repellent and nihilistic. Many critics linked the film to an infantile reading of Nietzsche, which further raised the spectre of the Nazis and helped endorse the view that *Fight Club* was politically dangerous and morally repugnant. However, critical opinion was split, with some reviewers seeing *Fight Club* as a brilliantly effective critique and biting satire of contemporary life.

The film created censorship issues for the BBFC who insisted on minor cuts to two scenes of fighting. These have subsequently been reinserted as the BBFC's guidelines have become more tolerant of adult-orientated material.

In 1999 the fear of the 'Millennium Bug' was indicative of a general anxiety over many aspects of Western culture. These were focused on notions of gender and in particular male anxiety of emasculation and feminisation. Generation X showed its disdain for the baby-boomers when Woodstock 2 descended into violent farce. The Columbine massacre heightened this sense of generational mistrust and unease.

In 1999 a new breed of film-makers announced their presence with a number of groundbreaking films. Their films were stylistically adventurous and technically complex. They were films that had as much in common with the internet, computing, gaming and music video as they did with old Hollywood or European art cinema. A new cinematic generation was emerging, many of whom would become key players and major creative forces in the first decade of the twenty-first century.

Chapter 4: Interpreting *Fight Club*

The interpretation of a film text invariably relies on the application of theory. Theory acts as a set of spectacles: looking at the world through its lenses sharpens focus, magnifies detail and clarifies understanding. Good theories have general application and predictive potential. An awareness of the many theoretical approaches underpins a more advanced study: without theory we are blind.

Studying *Fight Club* has been building towards a theoretical interpretation of *Fight Club* and has already referenced a number of possible theoretical positions, such as postmodernism and feminism. We will now explore these and other interpretive positions in more depth. However, it should be noted that such philosophical digressions are by their very nature also open to debate, something really beyond the scope of this guide. The reader is asked, therefore, to accept that the critical positions presented below are merely broad characterisations and do not reflect the rich diversity of possible interpretations. For example, it is deeply problematic to simply categorise a theoretical approach as 'feminist', as feminism is more than a mere caricature of empowered womankind: there are many positions on the wide spectrum of feminist theory. Indeed, the potent political and psychological nature of feminist studies lends itself to influence from other equally varied theoretical positions, such as Marxism or postmodernism. My point is that, with regards to *Fight Club*, I will merely point the reader in the general direction of a broadly characterised interpretation but will not significantly interrogate that position.

Auteur Theory

One of the most broadly understood, if not universally accepted, theoretical approaches in film studies is that of auteur theory: an auteur is here defined as a film-maker with a significant body of work whose films (often made within a variety of industrial, generic and cultural contexts) are illustrative of an idiosyncratic identity and a consistent approach to style and theme. An auteur of film has therefore a signature and this signature is manifest in the majority of their films. David Fincher is often talked of as an auteur. He is, it is suggested, a film-maker with a consistent personal vision who, no matter who the paymaster and what the brief, strives to realise that vision.

Any auteur study of Fincher should first make some comment on his advertising and music video work. It is in these time-limited, creatively adventurous arenas that Fincher developed, to paraphrase the title of Swallow's book, his 'dark eye'. Swallow goes on to broadly describe Fincher's auteur credentials:

> ...his films run the range from thriller to horror, from suspense to science fiction, from drama to black comedy ... he takes us on a journey into realms that lie half-glimpsed off the tangent of the real world ... a maverick amid the Hollywood mainstream ... [his stories] ... live, both literally and metaphorically, in the shadows. (Swallow, 2004, p.7)

Critics of Fincher reveal their own prejudices when deriding his commercial 'small screen' background, often viewing his work as technically proficient but lacking emotional depth. Fincher's dark vision is, to some detractors, the product of a technician's eye, an eye more concerned with complex camera blocking, intricate CGI and varied film stock rather than character development and emotional journeys. On such a reading, Fincher's feature films are merely exercises in style, lacking substance. However I think to accuse Fincher of a cold directorial style in films like *The Game* and *The Social Network* is to mistake precise observation for lack of interest and, as for *Fight Club*, to claim that its style dominates its substance is again to mistake invention for idle play. Fincher is a technician but one with a deep interest in the stories, which his technical expertise helps bring to life. As he himself notes in reference to both the stylist and auteur label:

> You're working to make yourself obsolete ... I don't like the idea of having a style, it seems so scary. It's so weird – what is it that makes your style? It's the things that you fuck up as much as the things that you do well, so half your style is stupid mistakes that you consistently make. (Swallow, 2004, p.31)

Fincher does not have an academic film background and responds to the auteur tag with the understandable gut reaction of any artist thus labelled. But he is being disingenuous here. He is renowned for his meticulous preparation and attention to detail and is the kind of artist to demand perfection. The 'mistakes' he therefore makes are themselves the product of a lengthy planning process or aspects of the film he loses control of. As he notes (ibid, p.30) on the process of directing: '[it's] thinking the thing up, designing all the sets and it's rehearsals and then the creative process is over. Then it's just war. ... It's 99 percent politics and one percent inspiration.' The scars of *Alien 3* run deep.

An academic work by Mark Browning (2010), *David Fincher: Films that Scar* concludes with the following observation (p.177): 'To a greater or lesser extent, all of Fincher's films are structured around a central dynamic pairing – [Tyler and Jack; Alien and Ripley, etc] ... in effect following one of his favourite films ... *Butch Cassidy and the Sundance Kid*.' Browning goes on to note that '[Fincher's] extreme ... obsessive, planning and execution of shots puts him closer to Hitchcock, especially in his meticulous preparation to the point where actors can seem incidental' (ibid.). This point is further illustrated in the *Fight Club* DVD commentary where Fincher admits to suffering extreme discomfort when filming love scenes. To him, unlike Hitchcock, actors are not cattle, but they are clearly a messy encumbrance. Browning further notes that: 'When Fincher's obsessive attention to detail does not lose sight of its audience, we have *Fight Club*, but when it does, we have *Benjamin Button* and parts of *Zodiac*. ... [At such times] emotional engagement with character and action seems to be secondary to extending technological possibilities' (2010, p.180).

Fincher's technical experimentation, it seems, is both his boon and his bane, but he can modulate his approach as in *The Game* and *The Social Network*. What still makes *Fight Club* his career-defining work to date is the perfect marriage of script to technique. Jack's cynicism, Tyler's scene stealing tub-thumping, Marla's frazzled compassion, Palahniuk's prescient observations and Fincher's bravura set pieces form a perfect combination. In *Fight Club*, at the very least, Fincher made a film where 'his style is the substance of his art' (Browning, 2010, p.177).

But what exactly are these stylistic flourishes? On the DVD commentary to *Fight Club*, Pitt and Norton gently mock Fincher's use of a very rich darkness, a velvety dense black that Fincher first used in *Se7en*. Fincher is, as we have seen, meticulous in his preparation from very early on in the pre-production cycle and no more so than when involved in bringing *Fight Club* to the screen. He is a virtuoso with slow, forward-moving crane shots and the possibilities of long takes. He is fascinated by the potential of the film camera, film stock and the technology of digitised film-making. His CGI work is renowned and at times ground-breaking: this was first seen in *Fight Club*'s costly opening and closing sequences and continued to develop with the even more complex and expensive *Curious Case of Benjamin Button* (2008). *The Social Network* showed a mature Fincher at his subtle best, seamlessly linking stunning CGI with plain drama through the replication of the Winkelvoss twins. He is renowned for shooting many takes but also using 'found footage' shot without the actor's knowledge: in *Fight Club* when Norton is at a business meeting and grimaces at a work colleague, showing off his bloody gums, he is actually looking at Fincher in an unscripted, supposedly off-camera, aside.

But what can be said of Fincher's themes and values? As with Palahniuk, who earlier noted that his fiction occupied the fringes of society, the same can be said of Fincher: his largely male protagonists are often ill at ease with their worlds. 'Little men' are something of a recurring feature: the social inadequate taking on the system – something which runs from *Alien 3*, via *Fight Club* right up to *The Social Network* and *The Girl with the Dragon Tattoo* with their 'revenge of the nerd' subtext. Noir themes also interest Fincher, as seen most spectacularly in *Se7en* and *Fight Club*: in the latter we find a voice-over, a *femme fatale*, a criminal underworld, and a shadow-filled city at night – all classic noir tropes. *The Girl with the Dragon Tattoo* plays on similar ideas with its neo-noir themes and marginalised central character. Clearly, then, some recurring thematic and evaluative aspects of Fincher's work do suggest a dark vision is regularly present: a baleful, sometimes ironic vision of humanity living dangerously at the fringes of society. And yet some of his films also hint at a future realignment with the mainstream, as the redemption narratives in *The Game* and *Fight Club* suggest. The leap from *Fight Club* to the *Social Network* is suddenly very small and Fincher's dark vision is shown to be one that is not necessarily pessimistic: from out of the chaos often a new order emerges.

So is Fincher an auteur? Following the definition used above, we might conclude that he is. Kevin McCormick, an uncredited producer of *Fight Club* and former Executive VP at Fox 2000 clearly feels that he is:

David is one of the only directors who can tell you two years before he's shot a scene exactly what you'll get when he's through. I remember going to the set two years to the day from when he described a tricky hard to visualize scene and there it was, down to the note. I got chills. Usually a director's vision is so diluted by other factors: collaborators, schedules, that sort of thing. Not David's. (DVD booklet, 2006)

Browning eulogises even more effusively about Fincher's directorial approach, going as far as to cite Nietzsche in terms of Fincher himself, rather than the more commonly referenced *Fight Club*: '...there is a certain "will to power" in an aesthetic context, not for personal gain or in any criminal sense, but to ascend new artistic levels in an individual film and in the art form itself' (2010, p.178).

Moral Panics and Media Effects Theory

Moral panics are cultural and social events, which, when negatively and hysterically misrepresented in the mass media, provoke emotive public debate, a powerful sense of moral outrage and the fear of social decline. As the panic deepens, the establishment often rushes through draconian legislation to resist the perceived degeneration in standards and values. A further feature of this generalised mood of public anxiety is that specific minority groups deemed responsible for the moral collapse are demonised and persecuted. At its most extreme, this persecution can result in imprisonment, abuse and victimisation. Moral panics often arise at a time of social division and change, and the demonised, marginalised group is frequently blamed for wider social problems. In terms of youth-orientated cultural products that lead to moral panics, such as pop music or video games, there is often a sense that the product is representative of a more general 'problematic' youth culture: a morally and physically dangerous culture which is 'running wild'. The elements of such a culture could find further expression in the use of drugs and the practice of other illegal activities, as well as in more generally expressed 'negative' attitudes and values. All of this can run counter to the mainstream culture and further exacerbate the reactive feelings associated with a moral panic. The combined effect creates the idea that an element of society is 'out of control' and needs to be urgently suppressed or even eradicated before things 'get out of hand'.

That *Fight Club* led to a moral panic is clear from some of the more vituperative reviews cited earlier. The nature of this panic was not, however, down to the perceived political or philosophical radicalism of the film but rather its treatment of violence – something that we have seen was misguidedly chosen by the film's distributors as its unique selling point. *Fight Club* was keyed into its time in that the anxiety over the increased mediation of culture and the increasing proliferation of violent imagery and language in that media immediately created a strong negative response to the film. A number of films released in the 1990s had already led to fierce oppositional press campaigns and even eventual censorship, none more famous than *Reservoir Dogs* (Tarantino, 1992) and *Natural Born Killers* (Stone, 1994). Then there was the violent tendency of male-targeted video games like *Mortal Kombat* (1991) and the stereotypically violent nature of music such as rap, punk and heavy metal, all of which contributed to a heightening of tension with regards to cinematic depictions of violence – especially when the films had strong youth appeal.

It was within such a climate that *Fight Club* failed to find many friends on its original release. From a frosty and misjudged premiere at the 1999 Venice Film Festival, coming up against intense millennial tension, generational unease with the internet boom and finally the civic calamity of the Columbine massacre, it is at least understandable that so many people misjudged the comic and satirical intent of the film on its release.

Lying behind many moral panics is a theoretical debate called 'effects theory'. Put simply, this is a theory which suggests that media products such as films can and often do affect their audiences or users. The nature and impact of the effect is still open to debate and little compelling empirical evidence actually exists to favour one theory over another. It is largely for this reason and the emotive character of the debate that moral panics arise.

At one end of the spectrum of effect theory we find the idea that media audiences are passive 'couch potatoes' and so vulnerable. Show such people violent films, the argument goes, and they will themselves become violent. There is, therefore, a direct relationship between the content of a media product and the audience's behaviour and moral compass (sometimes referred to as hypodermic theory). Taking the audio-visual depiction of violence as an example, the audience can also become so used to on-screen depictions that they cease to have an impact on them, so that on-screen and, critically, off-screen violence, become normalised (desensitisation theory). Another theory argues that the audience, especially a very young one, may merely copy what they see (copycat theory). Or perhaps the audience may develop a value system through their allegiance or admiration of cultural gatekeepers; if Brad Pitt says it is cool to fight then maybe it is (two-step flow theory). These various passive effects models are often invoked when an 'off-the-shelf' explanation is needed for a shocking event, such as the infamous 1993 murder of toddler James Bulger by two schoolboys in Liverpool. During the trial of his murderers, the malign effect of the film *Child's Play 3* (Bender, 1991), found at the home of one of the killers, was cited as a contributory factor in their actions and this led to a review of the 1984 Video Recordings Act – despite the fact that investigating police offers in this case explicitly rejected this link and, indeed, made clear there was no evidence that the boys had even seen the film. Proponents of the theories at the passive end of the effects spectrum are often characterised as politically reactionary and conservative; they typically favour tighter controls on regulation in terms of censorship and classification and see the cultural world as a battleground with clearly demarcated lines of conflict, often generational or class-based.

At the other end of the effects spectrum sits the broad theory termed 'uses and gratification theory'. Here, the model of effect views the audience as aware, intelligent and active. The audience actively and consciously uses mediated products in ways that fulfil specific needs and pleasures. Followers of such a position often argue for a liberal, broad-minded approach to censorship and classification and tend to see the cultural world as a playground that lacks clear divisions and rules.

So is *Fight Club* a battleground or a playground? As we saw earlier, certain Christian film watchdogs like Screenit clearly identify this film with a broader moral decline and by using a passive model of effects theory argue for the strict censorship of its dangerously attractive material. Conversely, we have also seen that the film-makers, the artists and producers behind the film, broadly see *Fight Club* as an intelligent satire and black comedy. The danger for them rests in the film's radical themes, not in its violent content. Equally important for them is the principle of freedom of artistic expression and social commentary, a democratic principle that is too often jettisoned by critics with a battleground mentality. Edward Norton, in particular, has been outspoken on this issue, as can be seen from the following quotation where he defends the violence in *Fight Club* in terms of its artistic intent:

> I think that any culture where the art is not reflecting a really dysfunctional component of the culture is a culture in denial. And I think that's much more intensely dangerous on lots of levels than considered examinations of those dysfunctions through art is dangerous. ... I think that it is a very appropriate discussion to ask what are the ways in which the presentations of violence affect us. I'm not going to say I get particularly disturbed by many, but I would aim those questions more at films that present violence in a way that it is presented as entertainment or where violence is made an aesthetic in its own right.

> I think that there's a legitimate question as to how certain presentations of violence ... affect us all. But I don't think that the violence that is in our culture means that art shouldn't examine that violence. I think that if we were to refrain from serious examinations in art of any kind of ways in which we're unhealthy or ways in which we're dysfunctional as a culture, ... we wouldn't have most of the things we point to as landmarks in our cultural landscape. Nabokov shouldn't have written *Lolita* out of fear that an old man would go and molest a young girl. Scorsese should have never made *Taxi Driver* and the Beatles shouldn't have written *The White Album* because Manson can use it as an outlet for his pathologies. (Yale University interview, 1999)

As with the study of the horror genre, exploring our fears can tell us a lot about ourselves. Those monsters in the cellar, Norton suggests, are ourselves, and we deny them at our peril.

Political Theory

Fight Club's Left and Right

As we saw earlier in the reviews by Roger Ebert ('cheerfully fascist') and Alexander Walker ('resurrects the Führer principle'), certain reactions against *Fight Club* were based on the film's perceived right-wing politics.

The film, some argued, takes a dramatic and downward turn with the formation of Project Mayhem. The space monkeys become barely disguised Nazis and Tyler Durden is elevated to the status of Hitler: an autocrat who dominates his disciples and victims alike with charisma, emotive propaganda and the threat of violence. Tyler's soap is culled from the bodies of the rich just like (so legend has it) the Jews were farmed for their body parts in the death camps. Tyler and Jack dehumanise new recruits to their Project by physically and verbally abusing them ('You are not special'), shaving their hair and forcing them into a uniform, placing them in barracks (the basement dorm at Paper Street), making them do menial work and even banning their names. Only when they die are the space monkeys allowed names ('His name is Robert Poulson'). In short, a private army is formed and run by Jack and Tyler, who are now called 'Sir!' by the recruits. There are further similarities between the Nazis and Project Mayhem: both groups aim to destabilise society through orchestrated propaganda, violence, vandalism and destruction. Project Mayhem's division into various departments is symptomatic of a rational approach to political and social transformation: 'Arson meets Monday. Assault on Tuesday. Mischief meets on Wednesday. And Misinformation meets on Thursday. Organised chaos. The bureaucracy of anarchy.' (Palahniuk, 2006, p.119).

Just like the Nazis, a bureaucracy of terror is established that enables its elitist leaders to enact brutalising transformations on the people. The so-called 'human sacrifices', as typified by that of the hapless store-clerk Raymond K. Hessel, are something that Tyler has been systematically perpetrating on citizens: the briefly glimpsed back of his bedroom door is covered with numerous identity cards taken from those 'sacrificed'. Finally, we have the sense that history is a failure and for the modern world to emerge a cleansing process needs to take place: Tyler's desire to destroy the ideologically polluted past (credit records in the film and the National Museum in the novel) is nothing less than the Nazi brown-shirts burning books.

Henry Giroux, an outspoken critic of the film, notes that it is: '[a] morally bankrupt and reactionary film. Representations of violence, masculinity, and gender ... seem all too willing to mirror the pathology of individual and institutional violence that informs the American landscape, extending from all manner of hate crimes to the far right's celebration of paramilitary and proto-fascist subculture' (Giroux, 2001). Jesse Kavadlo, in an essay on Palahniuk's fiction, opines a different view: 'The book's political subtext, far from right wing, insinuates that our cherished bastions of American liberty – the free market, liberal autonomy, and family values – come loaded with nascent totalitarianism' (J. Kavadlo, 2008).

Perhaps Ebert, Walker and Giroux are onto something. Perhaps *Fight Club* is wishfully evoking a desire for strong leadership and an end to woolly liberalism. Or perhaps Kavadlo is right and it is the paradox of fascism inherent in capitalist liberalism that is the narrative's real target. It is thus easy to see why both ends of the political spectrum were enraged by the film: right-wingers fearing the individualistic anarchy and nihilism of its first half; left-wingers loathing the cultish militarism and tyranny of its last half. Browning suggests that this means *Fight Club* is 'politically muddled': 'As a light-hearted satire of specific aspects of consumerism, therapy culture, or disenfranchised masculinity the film works well, but the second half loses focus' (2010, p.104).

It might be helpful to look more closely at what the film and the film-makers actually say about its politics. We have already seen that in terms of genre there is not much agreement but Fincher and the cast were working largely under the assumption that they were making a dark comedy, a drama of male maturation, a left-field love story and a satire of contemporary life – but not really a text that argues strongly for any one specific political stance. Swallow quotes Fincher:

> I don't see the film as a condemnation of capitalism ... but I do think it's a definite condemnation of the lifestyle seekers, the lifestyle sellers and the lifestyle packagers. People misread a lot of what happened in *Fight Club* as some sort of anarchist recruiting film, and really, I don't think the movie really promotes any specific answers. (2004, p.141)

Fincher's remarks could be being directed against the authors of an essay on *Fight Club*'s politically anarchic character who state that:

> The similarities between anarchism and *Fight Club*'s philosophy are remarkable. Both arise among the working-class poor and rage against capitalism and the authorities that promote [it]. The anarchists and members of Project Mayhem use ... propaganda by the deed (and dynamite) to awaken the social consciousness of the masses. Most

importantly, they are both reacting to a gross financial imbalance resulting in the oppressive enslavement of the masses by their current power structure. (Chandler and Tallon, 2008)

Fight Club's Inner Space

So what is the political target of *Fight Club*? Fincher notes that, 'I always saw the violence in this movie as a metaphor for drug use ... [Jack] has a need. ... You're talking about a guy who's been completely numb. And he finally feels something and becomes addicted to that feeling' (Swallow, 2004, p.140). To rail against the political leanings of *Fight Club* is then to read the film too literally. It is to confuse what the film 'depicts' with what it 'prescribes'. It is dangerous to forget the messy narrative at the expense of its lurid representations.

Jack is a confused, depressed and emotionally numb insomniac. Jack has issues. He cannot relate with humans in a normal situation – beyond scenes of his morally repugnant work and alienating office life. We witness him metaphorically and literally 'in transit', lost in a 'single-serving', sterile world of hotel rooms and airports. When not working he spends time in his apartment – browsing IKEA catalogues and starring at the TV like a zombie. His fridge, like his soul, is empty and lacking substance. Indeed Tyler too is at first a mere phantom, flicking on and off through a number of subliminal appearances which only we see. This suggests that Tyler is literally being created out of the emotional and spiritual furnace of Jack's psychic breakdown – a manifestation of everything Jack unconsciously admires but consciously rejects. It is therefore significant that the very first subliminal glimpse of Tyler presages the discovery of the cathartic effect offered by therapy groups: when Jack's doctor, resisting Jack's pleas for prescription narcotics, ironically tells Jack that it is at such groups that he will witness the real meaning of pain, Jack is hooked, and Tyler is conceived.

The arrival of Tyler in the first of his subliminal manifestations is evidence of Jack's narrative need for someone to admire but it also serves to wake us up as spectators: as Jack slips further into a schizoid world we are forced to actively engage in the often passive experience of watching a film. Tyler's appearance is also a reminder that we are literally inside the mind of a mad man. The film starts inside that mind, inside the fear centre of Jack's brain, and we watch his synapses and neurones fire at the terror he feels. We alone can see Tyler – the doctor and Jack do not: ours is then an objectively viewed insight into a subjective experience. What we see must therefore be understood in those terms. Jack's frustrations are real and their causes are real too: as Fincher says, it is the 'lifestyle seekers and sellers' who are the villains of Jack's 'everyman' tale. It is the vapid consumer culture of late-twentieth century Western society that is the real target of the film: the subsequent fascistic character of Project Mayhem is merely the deranged fantasy of a powerless man desperately trying to gain control of his bifurcated self. The Project soon overpowers Jack (such is its reprehensible nature) and Jack eventually realises that he does not need disciples (fight club), a god (Tyler) or the IKEA catalogue to become fulfilled.

Fight Club and Jackass

Project Mayhem is, then, a politically naive invention and reflects Jack's political alienation: this man may well be a product of an alienating political system but he seems relatively uninterested in current affairs and popular culture. His avid studying of the IKEA catalogue while using the toilet is an unsubtle metaphor for a ravenous but unsatisfying desire for unfulfilled consumption. What he consumes produces moral constipation. Jack is literally and metaphorically 'full of shit' and the film details his wake-up call (and perhaps ours) but it does not articulate a deeply theorised political philosophy. If anything, the direct action and consciousness raising pranks of the Project presage two other events – one political and one cultural.

Project Mayhem identifies both the political frustrations that lead to terrorism and the cultural forces that lead to prankster TV and films: it is no surprise that over ten years on from the formation of Jackass on TV, the film Jackass 3D was one of 2010's top-grossing films. The ever-present threat of terrorist activity also led the UK Government in 2010 to identify terrorism as one of the UK's greatest security threats alongside eco-disasters and war. Misguided or not, Project Mayhem touched a still very sensitive nerve.

Fight Club's Luddite Utopianism

An argument can be constructed suggesting that *Fight Club* highlights a primitive political philosophy known as Luddite Utopianism or anarcho-primitivism. Tyler states that he wants to return the world to 'Ground Zero' and that Project Mayhem will 'save the world by producing a cultural ice age: a prematurely induced dark age'. He later fantasises about hunting elk in the forests that in the future will have reclaimed the Rockefeller Center in New York. He wants to end civilisation and the great cultural legacy that supports it: a legacy symbolised by museum vaults and credit card company data banks. Tyler's war with the past is largely informed by his war with the future – modernism is his enemy.

We will explore this more fully in the following section on postmodernism but it is worth noting here that modernism is itself utopian – arguing for a technologically-driven future where progress and equality are realised on a global scale. Tyler does not support that view and decides to take up arms against modernist culture. His battle plan, as one might expect considering it is the plan of an alter ego given flesh, is chaotic and confused. Targets range from individual sacrifices or resurrections ('near-life experiences' as typified by that of Raymond K. Hessel) to the destruction of civic art, fake castrations of public officials, demagnetising rental video tapes, urinating into soup at restaurants, splicing pornography into family films at the cinema and, of course, setting up fight clubs. Only in the novel does Tyler kill someone in cold blood: never in the film. The final act of commercial apocalypse and the destruction of the credit card tower blocks is in itself a hugely elaborate prank – highly unlikely to achieve its aim. The collapsing towers are a statement, a line drawn in the sand but hardly the fall of the Bastille. And the failure of this final gesture reveals the naive political thinking of a Luddite Utopian. By smashing the old world order, Tyler hoped to usher in a new dawn, the dawn of a post-industrial, neo-hunter-gatherer culture.

But this is fantasy not politics. By throwing out the middle-class superficiality of IKEA lifestyles and heavily mediated metrosexual attitudes, Tyler also dispenses with the law and the arts and knowledge accumulated over millennia. A dark age is not dark just because there are no lights; it is dark because chaos and irrationality and superstition walk abroad. The Luddite's problem is that they hate the present and fantasise nostalgically about a utopian past to which they think they can retreat. The notion of a return to Ground Zero is as flawed as the idea that Ground Zero is a utopian Eden. This is black-and-white thinking and lacks the complexity of response needed for a hugely complex solution. Tyler's views are, at best, childish and at worst, mad. That his views are by no means unusual is exemplified in the case of the 'Unabomber'.

Fight Club and the Unabomber

The 'Unabomber' (as in 'university and airline bomber') is Theodore Kaczynski (1942 –), an American mathematician and terrorist who engaged in a USA-focused mail-bombing campaign from 1978 to 1995 that killed three people and injured twenty-three others. Kaczynski sent a letter to *The New York Times* on April 24, 1995 promising to stop bombing if his 50-page manifesto, *Industrial Society and its Future*, was published. Fearing further attacks and in the hope that his writing style would be recognised, the FBI approved publication. The manifesto begins with the assertion that, 'The Industrial Revolution and its consequences have been a disaster for the human race'. It goes on to consider the psychological consequences for individual life within the 'industrial-technological system', and suggests that this system has forced humans 'to behave in ways that are increasingly remote from the natural pattern of human behaviour'. To remedy this desperate state of affairs, Kaczynski calls for a 'revolution against technology'. This form of extreme belief is clearly allied to Luddite Utopianism or anarcho-primitivism, according to which the change of role from hunter-gatherer to farmer has created social division, rule by force and personal alienation. What is needed, it is being argued, is a return to the Eden of the uncivilised through the abandonment and/or destruction of mass-market industry and technology.

Clearly, there are parallels here with *Fight Club*, as discussed in Barry Vacker's essay 'Slugging Nothing', which appeared in the philosophical collection, *You Do Not Talk About Fight Club* (Schuchardt [ed.], 2008). As he notes: '...the revolution fictionalised in *Fight Club* is the same revolution theorised in The Unabomber Manifesto' (p.203). Modern culture has created unfulfilling and false lifestyle needs far removed from our true and essential biological needs, something typified by Jack's flat with its designer fridge bereft of food. Tyler/Jack confirms his idealised utopian vision for the future in the film: 'You'll hunt elk ... around the ruins of the Rockefeller Centre ... You'll wear leather clothes that will last you the rest of your life ... This was the goal of Project Mayhem, Tyler said, the complete and utter destruction of civilisation.'

There are, then, clear links between the Tyler and the Unabomber in terms of their avowed primitivism and their recourse to violence to achieve their aims. This political approach is, however, something I have hopefully already shown to be at best misleading and simplistic. It is a political position which the mature Jack ultimately rejects.

In my view, then, the political message of *Fight Club* lies in its characterisation of (a) the mechanism by which extremist political cults emerge and recruit and (b) the desire to re-engage with a reality that is otherwise heavily mediated and soporific. On such a reading, *Fight Club* is a political wake-up call but one that lacks a consistent political ideology. The film identifies a problem and hints at some possible solutions but by no means does it successfully argue that either *Jackass* or Al-Qaida is the way forward. Indeed, as these solutions are the product of a deranged person – Jack – they are clearly not the answer. So what is? I believe it is the humanism of Marla as the film's penultimate shot of Jack and Marla truly connecting finally indicates.

Psychoanalytic Theory

Today, Freudian theory is somewhat discredited or at least regarded sceptically. It is very complex and there are also numerous nuances to the theory arising out of its hybridisation with other theoretical positions such as feminism. However, there is still plenty of mileage to be gained from a brief consideration of Freudian theory as applied to *Fight Club*.

Freud's taxonomy of the mind remains a potent description of our interior world, despite its dubious scientific worth. It is therefore no surprise to find it frequently referenced in theoretical discussions of *Fight Club*. Freud's theory structures the human mind into three broadly interconnected mental fields: the Id, Ego and Superego. Very simplistically put, the Id represents our primal psychic urges. Babies are therefore largely Id: unconscious, unrepressed and narcissistic. When the baby wants to eat, the desire to consume consumes it. The Ego is home to our rational, conscious mind. It is the mind we regard as 'self'. (Thus, in common parlance, a selfish, self-centred person is an 'egotist'.) In terms of the Ego, if we want food, we start to work out where it is, and how much it will cost, and when we will have time to get it, and what kind of food we feel like eating, and so on. In the adult world, drugs and alcohol are examples of some of the devices used to alleviate the tension built up in the conflict between the Id and the Ego. This conflict is critical because behind it Freud locates the psychic pressure that leads to severe mental illnesses such as phobias, neuroses and psychoses. Freud argues that in underdeveloped egos, like Jack's, the Id (Tyler) can escape its social and parentally enforced repression and perhaps even come to dominate the Ego: at its extremes this could lead to intolerable psychic distress, perhaps even tipping the weak Ego into a psychotic world of split or multiple personality disorders. On such a reading, Tyler represents the psychic steam escaping from Jack's seething mental agony. Without Tyler, Jack would find life unendurable: Tyler is to Jack what 'Mother' is to Norman Bates in *Psycho*. The Superego is the world of ethical and evaluative pronouncements. It is a moralistic world, existing in and beyond our minds. The hungry human may apply moral decisions to their desire for food: perhaps they have promised the doctor to diet; perhaps they are fasting in observance of a religious edict; perhaps they are a sportsman and so conflicted by their professionalism; perhaps they are breaking the law by eating during a time of national rationing. Jack's need to believe in a moral code reflects the battle between his Ego and Superego. The authority figures in his life, such as his boss or the police, disappoint him and so he is ripe for exploitation by the Id monster Tyler who has uninhibited access to Jack's superego.

The most common Freudian theorising of *Fight Club* is however in terms of the Id and Ego. Jack has a weak Ego – perhaps down to his fatherless, mother-centred up bringing. (Feminist critics of Freud tend to concentrate on his undoubted sexism: he is after all the theorist behind the concept of 'penis-envy'!) Jack seems unable to relate in an honest way with adults and is therefore fundamentally immature – trapped in those early years of his social and psychic development when his fragile Ego tried to emerge from the base appetites of his Id. His only emotive contact with the world is in therapy groups, where he lives a lie to experience the truth: only in ersatz therapy can he communicate with a world that he is otherwise numb to. His adult life is a 'single-serving' existence. His condo is a shallow materialistic shell. His sex life is non-existent: like his friends he now masturbates mentally over the IKEA catalogue. Designer possessions are the new porn. His loneliness and alienation are so profound that when he does finally meet a woman he likes and whom, he unconsciously realises, likes him, he panics. Arising from this immediate panic and his long-term psychic distress, Tyler emerges. Jack's frustrated life and his desire for happiness and fulfilment fuels the psychic furnace within which Tyler is forged.

But is Tyler truly pure Id, as some commentators argue, or is he rather the Superego personified? Tyler as Id is most clearly witnessed in the fight clubs: there he and the other fighters personify the animal – the beast in man. Indeed it is suggested that fighting allows men to reconnect with their 'inner beast', a kind of psychic version of the Luddite Utopian's reductive approach – go back far enough and you connect with the truth. It is for this reason that *Fight Club* bears comparison with alter-ego fantasy/horror genre narratives typified by Jekyll and Hyde, the Hulk and the Werewolf. The violence that Tyler unleashes via Project Mayhem has a destructive, childlike quality – at times akin to a tantrum rather than a well-thought out act of political rebellion. Tyler's love-making with Marla is depicted as unrestrained and frenzied, bestial in its energy and perversity. And finally, as Tyler tells Jack, in what is maybe the Id's anthem: 'I look like you want to look. I fuck like you want to fuck. I am smart, capable and, most importantly, I am free in all the ways you're not.' But there is more to Tyler than this. He is not the Hulk, despite his musculature; nor is he the unrefined monster of Mr Hyde. He is more than a mere beast, despite his appetites and strength. He has a philosophy after all: if Tyler were just a *Jackass*/Hulk/Jekyll clone then he would never need to articulate a belief system to explain his wild and childish pranks. And so we must conclude that Tyler is, in fact, largely a Superego fantasy of Jack's. He is someone who is willing to forge his own value system in a world dominated by nihilism. As we have seen, the coherence of the values formulated by Tyler are problematic and confused but the point is that Tyler's emergence from a childish Id to an adult Superego is in fact a literal maturation. In *Fight Club*, Jack grows up via the fantasy of Tyler: he first unleashes his repressed Ego and then moulds his newly minted, powerful alter ego with a philosophy that enables him to find life fulfilling and meaningful. Tyler's superman and his moral code are rejected by Jack's newly empowered Superego. Jack destroys his avatar to become truly himself. Finally, Jack is secure within an Ego that enables him to both love himself (and Marla) and formulate a positive moral vision of a future of which both he and Marla will now happily be a part.

Gender Identity and Gender Relations

The most common theoretical interpretation of *Fight Club* concerns gender identity and gender relations. This is in part due to the audience's initial encounter with the film, which in its title and early marketing apparently reverts to an atavistic vision of men: men as warriors, men as fighters, men as testosterone-fuelled thugs who get things done by extreme physicality; men as active agents. On such a reading, *Fight Club* is merely another dumb action film and if that were the case the furore that followed its release would seem unmerited. But of course, as we have seen, *Fight Club* is not an action film, despite the enduring images of the fight club itself. What upset most commentators at the time of the film's release was the film's subversive, putatively nihilist tone and the mistaken assumption that it advocated violence as a source of pleasure – 'macho porn', according to Ebert. Even then it may have ruffled few feathers but the star presence of Brad Pitt and the national anxiety generated by the Columbine massacre served to demonise the film even before its release. This is old ground, however; what is new for us is the film's subversive treatment of gender. Some of the key instances in the film that deal specifically with gender follow:

- Although Jack's psychosis is in some sense 'all about Marla' she occupies much less screen time than Jack and Tyler. Indeed, when she is present she either rows with Jack or has sex with Tyler. We learn little about her and her motives remain obscure – unlike Jack we hear no monologues and unlike Tyler we are not blessed with any significant philosophies. Only in the novel do we glean that Marla's mother is a frequent user of liposuction and that Marla uses the fat siphoned from her mother to reconstruct her own features and identity. Marla is a world-weary neurotic; she is a dishevelled fag-hag; she is 'Audrey Hepburn on heroin'. She is lonely. She is unhappy (indeed, we rarely see her smile). She is suicidal. She is a thief: stealing clothing from laundromats and food from 'meals on wheels'. She is also, like Jack, 'a big faker', attending therapy groups for similar reasons to Jack, as a tourist of despair. According to Jack, 'Marla's philosophy of life is that she might die at any moment. The tragedy, she said, was that she didn't'. She is sexually voracious and not prone to idealising sex: the infamous line, 'I haven't been fucked like that since grade school' was a substitution for an even more alarming line from the novel, 'I want to have your abortion'. Marla is, in short, damaged.[1]

The only other women given dialogue in the film are glimpsed fleetingly: a female passenger on a plane, a caring therapist and Chloe, the sexually desperate, terminally ill cancer patient.

- Bob acts as a maternal presence in the first half of the film. Bob is the castrated body builder who has lost his testicles due to cancer and who is now producing so much oestrogen that he has grown breasts (referred to disparagingly by Jack as 'bitch tits'). It is between these fake male breasts that Jack first finds solace and learns to cry. His emotional release then allows him to 'sleep like a baby' and so in some sense Bob's maternal character provides nurture and safe haven for Jack. Later in the film, Bob rejects the feminised emotionality of the therapy groups for the violence of fight club. And when Bob next meets Jack, the breasts that once comforted him become smothering devices. Bob's gender crisis, and by extension Jack's, is highlighted by the name of the therapy group at which they meet – 'Remaining Men Together'. Bob eventually has to die: half man and half woman he has no place in the polarised world Tyler and Jack are trying to build.

- Tyler is an idealised man. He is a figment of Jack's collapsed ego. He is the poster boy Jack wants to be: muscular, dynamic, sexually successful, charismatic, good-looking, a leader, and so on. Who better to play that role than a male pin-up and Hollywood's most photographed star?

- A barely disguised homoerotic tension pervades the film. In particular, the fight club features muscular, semi-naked men grunting, sweating and grappling in a dark basement (a popular metaphor for the Id). Then again there are the scenes when Tyler and Jack are sharing house together, almost like lovers in their intimacy – Tyler hugging Jack on his return from work and fondly slapping his bottom, Tyler and Jack sharing a beer, Tyler and Jack in the bathroom casually chatting while Tyler bathes. Palahniuk has subsequently 'come out' as gay, so these scenes may well be retrospectively construed as gay fantasies. But then, as we have already seen, the film is really about learning to love yourself so that you can love others. And Tyler is Jack. Jack is Tyler. Indeed, Tyler is a fantasy that eventually has to be rejected and destroyed. Far from being a love interest, Tyler is a cancer that needs to be cut out.

- The movie ends with a man and a woman holding hands. Jack has saved himself and Marla from his dark fantasy creation. Men and women need each other.

A common criticism of the novel and film is that of misogyny. These views largely derive from a few statements by Tyler/Jack in terms of mothers and the unsympathetic portrayal of Marla. Tyler/Jack claim they are the product of fatherless relationships: indeed, theirs is a fatherless generation. Taken literally, this relates to a fatherless culture or, by reversal, an overtly feminised one. Lacking any real male models other than Armani underpants models (the bus scene), men either strive for metrosexual perfection or feel a failure. Their power has evaporated: somewhat like Bob, men have become culturally emasculated.

This idea of men in crisis is one that has been around for at least as long as feminism, suggesting that by rightly striving for some kind of female equality, modern women have destabilised the notion of male identity. More relevant to the gestation of *Fight Club* is the 'Iron John' movement' or 'Mythopoetic Men's Movement' of the early 1990s, formed in part by the poet and male activist Robert Bly. His most important work on this theme is *Iron John: a Book about Men* (1990), a prose study of a Brothers Grimm fairy tale, *Iron John*. Lance Morrow discussed this work of Bly's in a 1991 article in *Time Magazine*:

He talks about each male's lost 'Wild Man', that hairy masculine authenticity that began getting ruined during the Industrial Revolution, when fathers left their sons and went to work in the factories. The communion between father and son vanished, the traditional connection, lore passing from father to son. And with it went the masculine identity, the meaning and energy of a man's life, which should be an adventure, an allegory, a quest. Bly goes on to say that, 'You cannot become a man until your own father dies.' (Morrow, 1991)

Indeed, the absence of fathers seems to be a recurring theme of Bly's, as it is in *Fight Club*. His attempts to reconnect contemporary men with their authentic, wild selves found form in various male bonding camps involving drumming and story telling. On this point Morrow, further notes:

Perhaps the men's movement is a very American exercise … it has that quality of Americans making fools of themselves in brave pop quests for salvation that may be descendants of the religious revivals that used to sweep across the landscape every generation or so in the 18th and 19th centuries. The men's movement belongs as well to the habits of the '60s baby-boomers who tend to perceive their problems and seek their solutions as a tribe. A Bly theme lies there. The boomers are a culture of siblings. Their fathers are all dead. The '60s taught that the authority of fathers (Lyndon Johnson, the Pentagon, the university, every institution) was defunct. The boomers functioned as siblings without fathers. Is it the case that now, like Bly, they are looking for the vanished father in themselves? (ibid.)

Certainly that is what Jack is doing: seeking the moral compass and authority by which to steer his own life: trying to replace the literal and metaphorical father that abandoned him. In the preface to his *Iron John*, Bly provides us with the very creed that motivates Jack's search for a paternal identity:

We are living at an important and fruitful moment now, for it is clear to men that the images of adult manhood given by the popular culture are worn out; a man can no longer depend on them. By the time a man is thirty-five he knows that the images of the right man, the tough man, the true man which he received in high school do not work in life. Such a man is open to new visions of what a man is or could be. (Bly, 1990)

Even in 2010, the debate Bly helped initiate rumbled on, as evidenced by *The Sunday Times Magazine* leading with a cover story called 'Why are Men so Unhappy?'(27 November 2010). The feature lists a litany of statistics to highlight this crisis in male equanimity such as: 59 per cent of undergraduates are female and 40 per cent of men are depressed about jobs, work and money. Feature writer Robert Crampton further suggests that, 'some men now find themselves as isolated as any '50s housewife', and that, 'For many men the twenty-first century paradise of constant communication is closer to purgatory'. The suggestion is clearly in line with *Fight Club*'s premise and back in 1999 this would all have sounded even more pertinent: then, the debate was hot, sparked by a critically acclaimed, high-profile study from American, Pulitzer-Prize winning journalist and feminist academic, Susan Faludi. Her study, *Stiffed: The Betrayal of the American Man* was issued in October 1999 close to the release date of *Fight Club*. Early in the book (p.6), Faludi details the zeitgeist to which her study (and, of course, *Fight Club*) was a response. She refers to 'American manhood under siege' and then goes on to list some of the cultural phenomena associated with this crisis: 'militiamen blowing up federal buildings; abortion clinics and schoolyard shootings'. Less serious but no less invidious are other symptoms of male anxiety, such as: 'lap dancing emporiums; the boom in male cosmetic surgery; abuse of steroids; the bonanza of miracle hair-growth drugs and the brisk sales of Viagra.' Faludi continues by describing further social calamity deriving from the male identity crisis: 'endangered young black men in the inner cities; Ritalin-addicted white young boys in the suburbs; deadbeat Dads everywhere and the anguish of downsized male workers.' Pollsters, she notes, have identified a new male voting group, 'the angry white male' and 'Social psychologists had issued reports on a troubling rise in male distress signals like anxiety and depressive disorders, suicide and attempted suicides and certain criminal behaviours'. (Faludi, 1990)

The synchronicity between Faludi's project and the work of Palahniuk is staggering, as Laura Ziskin comments: 'I was stunned when the movie was about to come out and I started reading about Susan Faludi and *Stiffed*. I thought it was so amazing that she had been working on this for six years while Chuck Palahniuk was under a diesel truck in Portland writing, in his brilliantly hyperbolic way, about the same things Susan was researching' (DVD booklet, 2006).

Faludi and Palahniuk were in their own ways both commentating on the contemporary male condition. An interesting article by Diana Abu-Jaber in the online arts website Salon.com details Faludi and Palahniuk meeting at a book reading in 1999:

Susan Faludi was reading from her new book on the disappointed and disenfranchised modern American male, *Stiffed*, to a standing-room-only crowd... In the audience was Chuck Palahniuk, whose novel on the disappointed and disenfranchised modern American male, *Fight Club*, had just opened in its film version. Palahniuk said that *Stiffed* had had an immediate, almost visceral importance in his own life. 'I read it in one weekend,' he said enthusiastically, indicating that her depiction of modern male-ienation [sic] was right on target. Recently, the *Fight Club* author had himself become a poster child for Faludi's argument. Her observations on the male condition – that ratings, rankings and salaries have become the main measure of success for men, that men have become just as victimized by consumerism as women, and that our society is imprisoned by the notion that victory is everything – all zinged home for Palahniuk. (Abu-Jaber, 1999)

Faludi returned the favour and positively reviewed the film of *Fight Club* in *Newsweek*, as referenced below in the PRNewswire (October 17 1999):

Feminist author Susan Faludi writes in the current issue of *Newsweek* that the film *Fight Club* is the *Thelma & Louise* for today's men ... Faludi, a Newsweek contributing editor, writes that just as women made *Thelma & Louise* an anthem and a consciousness-raising buddy comedy, so *Fight Club* will do for men who are striking back in the gender war. Men will connect with lead character Jack because he rebels against 'a world stripped of socially useful male roles and saturated with commercial images of masculinity ... For men who are offered fewer and fewer meaningful occupations, beating each other up may seem like the one-thing guys can still do well. But ultimately Jack finds that violence leads him nowhere,' Faludi writes. ... 'When Jack sends the boys away in the final scene, and throws his lot in with the defiant, if deviant, woman he's been afraid to court, he seems poised finally to begin life as an adult man ... For men facing an increasingly hollow, consumerized world, that path lies not in conquering women but in uniting with them against the hollowness. In that way... *Fight Club* ends up as a quasi-feminist tale, seen through masculine eyes. In *Thelma & Louise*, the one cop who understands the women's struggle fails in the end to save them, and the two women holding hands careen off the cliff. In *Fight Club*, the man and the woman clasp hands in what could be a mutual redemption.' (PRNewswire, 1999)

Fight Club as a 'quasi-feminist tale' according to one of America's leading feminists? The non-profit American news web site, Motherjones.com, presses Faludi on this surprising (but, in my view, accurate) reading, in an interview from 1999:

> '*So what's a good feminist like you doing writing sympathetically about men?*'

> I don't see how you can be a feminist and not think about men. One of the gross misconceptions about feminism is that it is only about women. But in order for women to live freely, men have to live freely, too. Feminism has shown us that what we think of as feminine is actually defined by cultural messages and political agendas. The same holds true for men and for what constitutes masculinity. Being a feminist opens your eyes to the ways men, like women, are imprisoned in cultural stereotypes. ...

> The truth is that what feminism is asking for is exactly what men want in their own lives, which is not to be judged according to superficial and ephemeral and impossible-to-attain objectives. Men don't want to live in a world run on retail values any more than women do. Like women, they want to be needed and useful participants in society. They want to have real utility and to be engaged in meaningful work. (Halpern, 1999)

Finally, we have a slightly different nuanced reading from a *Time Magazine* article by Joel Stein: 'The Emasculation Proclamation' (October 25, 1999):

> Faludi had seen *Fight Club* the night before. She liked the film, noting how the violence spiraled out of control and the main character found redemption with a woman in a familial relationship. She called the movie '*Stiffed* on speed,' so I called Chuck Palahniuk, who wrote the novel *Fight Club*; he was several hundred pages ... into Faludi's book and already calling his story 'the fictionalized version of *Stiffed*'.

Faludi's reading of *Fight Club* is, I think, critical when considering a response to claims that the film is misogynist. Her work and Palahniuk's are clearly linked by contemporaneous commentators and by the authors themselves. Their mutual response to a zeitgeist within which both genders are in some sense in crisis (Faludi's previous work was 1991's *Backlash: The Undeclared War against American Women*) and their joint conclusion that the cause for this crisis is neither men nor women but rather a superficial culture dominated by exchange value and consumer ideologies are clearly points of agreement. *Fight Club* is therefore about the male and female rejection of a redundant culture, a culture that diminishes gender identity, rather than a text that exacerbates gender division.

Postmodernism

Fight Club both displays and reflects upon many hallmarks of postmodern thought such as: irony, self-reflexivity, hybridity, exhaustion, end of history, loss of identity and originality, consumerism, a collapse of faith in meta-narratives and essential truths. For example, we have Tyler's rejection of a sense of completion through continuous improvement. 'I say never be complete. I say stop being perfect. I say let's evolve ... Self improvement is masturbation. Now, self destruction...' This rejection of modernism's belief (a meta-narrative) in the necessity of progress and the essentialism of 'self improvement' is a classic postmodern tic.

Later, we find references to our culture lacking historical placement, making us literally 'dispossessed', in part due to an over-mediated immersion in the fantasy of advertising and marketing. Lacking no sense of time and place, we live in a permanent limbo of evanescent meaning: we are spiritually deadened by our encounter with a morally nihilistic consumerism. We are sold, and buy into, the mediated dream of fame and fortune. Tyler, in the end, notes that the postmodern condition is producing, in agreement with Susan Faludi, 'angry white males'. Tyler is furious and something must change.

Then we have the most frequently cited postmodern quotation from *Fight Club*: 'With insomnia nothing is real, everything is far away; everything is a copy of a copy of a copy.' Thus we are copies of copies of copies and our original reality, grounded in truth, has been lost to us. Even friendship is now characterised by this depthless quality. Our friends are really strangers: 'The people I meet on each flight, they are single-serving friends.'

Mass mediation has belittled and simplified us. Our 'uniqueness' as individuals is really just a creation of mass marketing: we are a market first and then an audience, we are ourselves at the very last, if at all. As Tyler notes, 'We're consumers. We're by-products of a lifestyle obsession. Murder, crime, poverty, these things don't concern me. What concerns me are celebrity magazines, television with 500 channels, some guy's name on my underwear.'

We are blurring the boundaries between truth and fiction, reality and illusion. We feel, in a way, that what we buy defines us: the dream can become a reality because there is now no difference between a dream world and our world. In such a place it makes absolute sense to ask whether a brand name is our name ('I'd flick through the catalogues and wonder what kind of dining set defines me as a person'). We want to nest in IKEA and look like young, beautiful fashion models. And just like we have been branded by the consumerist system, so too will our modernist dreams of deep space exploration: even the stars can be marketed, as Jack explains: 'When deep space exploration ramps up it will be the corporations that name everything: the IBM Stellar Sphere; the Microsoft Galaxy; Planet Starbucks.'

Jack and Tyler reject this depiction of an insubstantial postmodern world and so, despite Jack's cool irony, the self-reflexivity of Fincher's direction and his casting of the film star Pitt, the world must still change. *Fight Club* has too much heart to be truly postmodern. It is biting cultural satire with a desire to wake us up, and although Tyler is critical of mass marketing and soulless consumerism, he wants to initiate a return to a nostalgic agrarian utopia. Jack, on the other hand, wants to find himself by dispensing with the illusion of Tyler. Both Jack's and Tyler's desires are a far cry from the ironic humour of the postmodern condition. It is rather in their application of a Nietzschean ethic that we will find the true meaning of *Fight Club*.

Nietzsche

Nietzsche and nihilism and are both frequently cited in critical commentaries on *Fight Club*, although rarely in anything but laymen's terms. There is insufficient space here to fully develop a response, other than by dealing with their very specific common points of reference. Thus with regards to Nietzsche, the nineteenth-century German philosopher, the most common point of linkage with *Fight Club* is found via his concept of the 'übermensch' or, as it is inadequately translated into English, the 'overman' or 'superman'. In terms of nihilism, an ancient but complex philosophical position, *Fight Club* is largely critiqued for its endorsement of a moral and existential nihilism: the idea that there is no real meaning in life or in moral positions like 'good' and 'evil'. We will tackle both Nietzsche and nihilism together, as not only is Nietzsche's moral philosophy often falsely accused of being nihilist but it is in fact a direct response to the nihilism he diagnosed as infecting late-nineteenth century culture. In other words, Nietzsche and *Fight Club* have a lot in common, though not for the reasons often given.

Friedrich Nietzsche (1844–1900) is one of the most influential moral philosophers of the modern era. He remains one of Germany's most renowned thinkers and his ideas have been the subject of great controversy and varied interpretation. One reason for this is his tendency to write in a beautifully stylised, often poetic, way; another is the fact that although his thought is far from systematic, it is eminently quotable and at times deeply shocking. It is no surprise that this is the philosopher who famously announced that 'God is dead and we have killed him' (*The Gay Science*, 1883) and 'That which does not kill me makes me stronger' (*Twilight of the Idols*, 1888). A further complication to the mystique behind Nietzsche's ideas derives from the man himself: a brief working life ravaged by illness and tragic descent into madness and infirmity at the age of 44; a prolific but barely noticed publishing history, which only posthumously led to fame and finally, and most infamously, lionisation by the National Socialist Party or Nazis. This last point is the one most casual readers unfortunately still associate with Nietzsche, despite it being soundly debunked by most contemporary academics. Sadly for Nietzsche, after his illness and death, his sister Elizabeth became his trustee. Elizabeth was a fanatical nationalist and anti-Semite, who re-edited her brother's papers and curried favour with the Nazis, who then adopted some of Nietzsche's more acceptable ideas as their own. Certain key concepts like 'will-to-power', 'master/slave morality' and 'the übermensch' were seized on by the Nazis to back up their fascist politics and the cult of their leader, the Führer. Thus tarnished, it is only recently that Nietzschean scholarship has climbed from beneath the shroud of the death camps. That said, as we have seen, those critics of *Fight Club* who accuse the film of peddling a sub-Nietzschean philosophy have this dark Nazi association in mind and thus help promote a misreading of Nietzsche that is out-of-date, inaccurate and unmerited.

The unifying factor in Nietzsche's diverse thought is an attempt to understand the moral conditions that lead to the development of vital (healthy) cultures and decadent (unhealthy) cultures. Vital cultures can nurture a strong character able to formulate values. Nietzsche calls such a character 'the übermensch' (the 'superman') and his/her special ability is to invent new values and thus reject centuries of traditional thinking associated with ossified notions of good and evil, right and wrong. (One of Nietzsche's most important books is accordingly titled *Beyond Good and Evil* [1886].) A particular target of Nietzsche's was the value system of Christian morality (the dominant moral system of his age), which endorsed such virtues as humility, pity and meekness. Equally repellent to him was the mob-rule of modern democracy, with its tendency towards compromise and commonality. He was also concerned about scientific reductionism – the way science made that which is special and unique in humanity seem small and inconsequential. These cultural phenomena – Christianity, Democracy and Science – coupled with 'the death of God' were, according to Nietzsche, producing a decadent culture or, in other words, a nihilistic one: a culture without values and without the ability or strength to form new ones. In other words the meaning of our lives had become unstable thanks to Darwin and the loss of religious faith. Old certainties no longer rang true and this had led to a culture of existential anxiety: the anxiety of having to create meaning in a meaningless world. It is for this reason that the übermensch faces such a monumentally difficult task, perhaps even an impossible one. Indeed, the apparent impossibility of generating meaningful values has led some commentators to argue that Nietzsche is in fact a moral nihilist – but that is unfair, for Nietzsche has his übermensch. And even if he did not, mankind would have to evaluate: '[the] truth about human will, its *horror vacui*: it must have a goal – and it would even will nothingness rather than not will at all' (*On the Genealogy of Morality*, 1887, 3, 1). The 'nothingness' Nietzsche mentions here is essentially a rejection of this world for a transcendental world beyond – the cornerstone of Christian and indeed many other religious doctrines. Nietzsche opposes this and argues for a philosophy that is imminent, that engages with the world as it is, warts and all, rather than a philosophy that disengages with life and seeks solace in transcendental values that lie beyond us.

Another feature of Nietzsche's later work which can aid our understanding of *Fight Club*, is his explanation of the formation of moral values, something he wrote about most famously in *On the Genealogy of Morality*. It is in this book that the 'master/slave dichotomy' makes its most developed appearance. In short, Nietzsche argues that the masters (men and women) who noted their own power, and called it 'good', made the first moral evaluations. Later, the slaves rejected this evaluation and turned it on its head, making the weak and meek aspects of their characters 'good' and so making the pride, might and self-confidence of the masters, 'evil'. Weak or slavish characters are also subject to 'ressentiment' (a kind of poisonous repression adapted later by Freud), which is underscored by Nietzsche's concept of the 'Will to Power': a universally dynamic energy pervading all life and in human terms, manifest in the actual 'will'. Block the dynamic of the will's outpouring and we create the conditions of decadence, nihilism and ill health. In effect, dam a river and the water becomes stagnant. Nietzsche holds that reactive natures are sickly and perverse. By being unable to express themselves immediately and with force they are compelled to internalise their energies and this produces huge pressures within, energies which turn upon themselves and self-devour – literally self-harm. When the power is eventually released it is profoundly reactive in nature, vengeful and cruel. Alternatively, active natures, the masters and the übermensch, are expressive and creative. They may be harsh but they are not bitter – theirs is a natural energy, like that of a bird of prey.

The Nietzschean übermensch is not, however, an infallible manifestation of human perfection. Thus we find in *Beyond Good and Evil* (section 260, p.74): '… in all higher and more complex cultures there are also apparent attempts to mediate between the two moralities … sometimes even their violent juxtaposition – even in the same person, within one single breast.'

And later on in the *Genealogy*, '...there is perhaps no more decisive mark of the '*higher nature*' [Nietzsche's italics]... than to be divided against oneself in this sense and to remain a battleground for these oppositions' (p.35).

So it seems a 'higher nature' is one that is a battleground for the opposing master and slave moralities. In this sense, we can all be übermensch - or at least those of us who are willing to acknowledge the heaviest of truths (the truths that have value but which are unpalatable). In the subtitle of Nietzsche's final work, *Ecce Homo* (1888) we find the question that is really important to the übermensch: 'How one becomes what one is.' Become who you are! Nietzsche's elitist übermensch is nothing more than the human who knows what he or she is (physiologically as well as psychologically) and who is prepared to forge values accordingly. Such a task is plainly very hard and many will fail but Nietzsche asserts that the task is possible. Without such a possibility, we stumble towards 'suicidal nihilism' and succumb to ever more desperate attempts at transcendentalism. The 'truths' of this world lie in this world and Nietzsche invites us to embrace this. We need to form values but most importantly we need to form values that are in accord with our natures – that is the übermensch gospel. Despite accusations of elitism, Nietzsche's übermensch can now fruitfully be seen as a template for the self-actualising individual.

So – how does all this relate to *Fight Club*? It is interesting to think what Jack would have made of Nietzsche: Edward Norton, on the other hand, is no stranger to Nietzsche's work, as is evidenced by his frequent references to the philosopher in interviews about *Fight Club*. What is clear is that Jack regards himself as a slave – Tyler refers to the members of the first fight club as 'slaves with white collars'. Jack is clearly powerless and sickly. His heavily mediated life, with its shallow consumerist values and amoral business practices, has destroyed his sense of personal worth. Jack's subsequent depression and mental illness is a symptom of his descent into moral and existential nihilism. He is unable to find true meaning in his life and cannot endorse a moral scheme: only the pain of life seems to give him the opportunity to 'sleep like a baby'. Either he continues to slide into a suicidal nihilism or he must create new values and regain his power. But this is very, very hard (as Nietzsche noted) and Marla seems to merely complicate the issue. Jack is a deeply unhappy insomniac in abject denial of his true feelings: it is due to the huge pressures these conditions produce that Tyler flickers into existence. The four subliminal Tylers appear at times of stress and illustrate that Tyler is soon to emerge into Jack's life fully empowered. Tyler himself remarks at the end of the film, when Jack has realised they are the same person:

> You were looking for a way to change your life. You could not do this on your own. All the ways you wish you could be – that's me.

Tyler is therefore the active agent that Jack wants to be – but as he is Tyler, to grow he must do more than accept Tyler's master morality. As we saw above, in the most developed characters the master and slave moralities battle each other. That is exactly what is happening to Jack. But the masters, according to Nietzsche, while admirable and charismatic, are also truly monstrous. Tyler's moral evaluations are confused and unsystematic, as we have already seen. His valuations are rarely positive, often negative and nostalgic. It is for this reason that Jack has to eventually dispense with Tyler: his unrepressed cruelty is just too dangerous for Jack. His is the 'unifying consciousness' that eventually comes to terms with a new set of reformulated values – his love for Marla. Jack is therefore the übermensch who rejects Tyler's master morality and the slavish morality of Jack's old life.

Another Nietzschean analogy can be found seemingly paraphrased in one of Tyler's key expressions of his own philosophy - *I don't want to die without any scars*. This is akin to Nietzsche's idea of 'what doesn't kill me makes me stronger'. Indeed, according to Nietzsche, a life truly lived is an existentially difficult if not painful one. Tyler and Nietzsche want us to live life to the full, without the comfort of illusions. We need to face up to the reality of life and death and only then are we free to make choices. Such an experience will be tough and will scar us but we will emerge stronger for it.

Finally, there is the very Nietzschean idea of the death of God: God the Father. Our ultimate responsibility now derives from the fact that we are in charge. God's death is as much a death of excuses – we are now the masters of our own lives. Growing up means accepting personal responsibility and no longer trying to excuse our behaviour by blaming God. Tyler feels much the same way:

Our fathers were our models for God. If our fathers bailed, what does that tell you about God? ... You have to consider the possibility that God does not like you, he never wanted you; in all probability he hates you. ... We don't need him. Fuck damnation, man. Fuck redemption. If we're God's unwanted children – so be it ...

So is *Fight Club* a film that accords with Nietzsche, and, in particular, his vision of the übermensch: Tyler as superman? No. Nietzsche and Tyler agree on a kind of naturalistic realism and a determined, stoic acceptance of life. They are 'realists' in that sense: taking life as it is. They are also dismissive of conventional ideologies: going 'beyond good and evil'. But Tyler is no übermensch. He has no values to put in place once the destruction is over. He is a moral nihilist and so Jack does what Nietzsche would have done, he destroys nihilism. Jack, if anyone, is the übermensch. Tyler is a paramilitary propagandist, a narcissistic psychopath and cult leader who represents the true nihilism inherent in Jack's morally empty world. Nietzsche would have applauded Jack for his courageous destruction of Tyler.

Conclusion

Fight Club remains an important and influential film text. It is still controversial thanks to the enduringly radical character of both its form and content. *Fight Club* is a modern classic with a mission to change the world. Whether you can answer the rhetorical question posed by The Pixies' song at the end of the film is the point of the film: 'Where is your Mind?' Whether you can answer that question, once Jack destroys his monstrous creation, Tyler, and the buildings start toppling, is the true meaning and power of the film. It is time to wake up and know exactly where you are. As Tyler exclaims when he and Jack clamber from the wreckage of their intentional car crash: 'That was a near-life experience.' Their human self-sacrifice in that scene shows *Fight Club* is a narrative of emotional maturation and community. It is, truly, all about Marla.

I began this guide by comparing *Fight Club* to Nietzsche's late work, *Twilight of the Idols* (1888). Like the film, our journey has returned us to the beginning. My point is that *Fight Club* (and, for that matter, Nietzsche) is ultimately about personal and cultural transformation. *Fight Club* is dynamite and knowing that can really help when we explore its appeal. To some (and I include myself in this category) the film is stylistically, technically and ideologically radical. It feels like its message is really important. It is good dynamite. It is the kind of explosive charge needed to clear away the debris of a failed civilisation and construct the building blocks of a new age. On the last page of the novel we find this quote: 'We're going to break up civilisation so we can make something better out of the world.' *Fight Club* is still a text we need because it shows us that the demolition can't begin until we know ourselves better.

Fight Club - good dynamite?

Footnotes

1. In the USA, students attend 'grade school' between the ages of 5 and 14. It seems that Marla's approach to sex has long been subversive.

Chapter summary

Auteur Theory: Despite being an effective collaborator, Fincher is clearly an auteur. His meticulous preparation and involvement in all aspects of the film-making enterprise illustrates a need for control over the medium, which was no doubt further focused by his negative experience on *Alien 3*. Fincher seems interested in critiques of contemporary life that focus on marginalised characters and criminality. He is also a groundbreaking user of CGI. He has therefore an idiosyncratic treatment of theme and style that merit the accolade of 'auteur'.

Moral Panics and Media Effects Theory: *Fight Club* was released into an atmosphere of moral panic, due to its perceived celebration of reckless male violence. The BBFC in particular reacted to this mood by cutting certain violent scenes; significantly, the mood has now changed and the cuts have been restored. Hollywood and many leading film critics also reacted negatively to the film and so fuelled the moral panic. Aside from the cultural anxieties surfacing in 1999 and the deeply shocking Columbine massacre, commentators also used simplistic models of media effects to further stigmatise the film. Over ten years since its release, *Fight Club* is now seen as a modern cult classic and the anxiety over its content seems now very much an over-reaction.

Political Theory: *Fight Club* presents an example of anarcho-primitivism or Luddite utopianism, given form by Tyler's fictional Project Mayhem and contextualised by the very real 'Unabomber'. The aim of both is to violently end civilisation as we know it and return us all to a pre-industrial, pre-technological simplicity. In such a world we will find the utopian culture we all seek – a kind of harmonious hunter-gatherer existence. This is, of course, a hopelessly idealised and reactionary political philosophy and as such it is parodied in *Fight Club* rather than endorsed. The film ends with Jack rejecting the cult of Tyler and his space monkey followers. What matters, as the film's final scene shows, is that we remain together. Our culture's problems are therefore remedied through community rather than the chaos of anarchic destruction and the idealised celebration of a new primitivism.

Critics who read into the film evidence of a latent desire for fascism or a communist rejection of capitalism are also reading too much into the subjective mental breakdown of our main protagonist, Jack/Tyler. The film is a powerful critique of a superficial consumer culture and the moral vacuum created by consumers who buy into that superficiality but this is not necessarily anti-capitalist. The emptiness of brand identity and the rapacity of multinational corporations are parodied but capitalism is not necessarily under attack. However, fascism is shown to derive its power from the cult following of a powerful leader by the weak and nameless. That this eventually leads to death and destruction is meant to shock both Jack (and us) into the realisation that this too is an untenable political approach. *Fight Club* is anticorporate, anti-consumer and anti-brand but not anti-capitalist. *Fight Club* shows anarcho-primitivism to be an immature political philosophy, which is ultimately rejected for a less radical humanism. The cult of paramilitary fascism is shown to be empty and dangerous, and it is powerfully rejected in the film.

Psychoanalytic Theory: Tyler is, at first appearance, the beast of the Id unleashed. Equally, he can be read as the Superego that Jack needs to be whole – the father-figure guide who imposes upon him moral strictures. However, Tyler as unrepressed Id is compelling, in particular as he clearly engages in the base needs that Jack cannot bring himself to experience – wild sex with Marla being but one appetite of the Id that Tyler is more than happy to satisfy on behalf of Jack. Indeed, Jack's multiple personality disorder may also be read in terms of Jekyll and Hyde – Tyler as Hyde is that part of us all which if uncontrolled or unrepressed (to use Freud) becomes an amoral monster. On such a reading, Jack does not destroy Tyler; he merely develops enough ego strength to repress him. Hyde is sent back to the primitive psychic interior and Jack can now engage with society secure in himself and guided by a moral code he believes in.

Gender Identity and Gender Relations: Gender remains the most critically appraised aspect of *Fight Club*. The film clearly can be read as an exploration of male identity in crisis: something that most recently found expression in America with the ideas of Robert Bly and the 'Iron John' movement and subsequently through the work of Susan Faludi. Some feminist critics find the film misogynistic and others see it as a homoerotic text. I (along with Faludi and Palahniuk) have argued that it is neither and that in fact the film presents women as an essential and equal element in the humanist redemption of man. *Fight Club* is really 'all about Marla'.

Postmodernism: On one level *Fight Club* is clearly a postmodern text in that it is a self-reflexive, ironic, generic hybrid, with disdain for authority and convention and essentialist identities. However, I do not believe it embraces the postmodern condition but rather critiques it, looking towards a more positive future where the nihilist tendencies of postmodernity ('anything goes') are rejected.

Nietzsche: Critics of *Fight Club* seeking analogies with Nietzsche often mistakenly lean on fascistic interpretations of his work. This is a mistake, as neither *Fight Club* nor Nietzsche can successfully be interpreted, as Alexander Walker might have it, as 'paradigms of the Hitler state'. On the contrary, both *Fight Club* and Nietzsche can be read as studies of a difficult and sometimes painful maturation process: a process of personal empowerment that rejects any suggestion of the cult of the leader. I interpret Nietzsche's übermensch (superman) as a person (much like Jack) who struggles to define a moral code that is theirs, rather than one that is imposed upon them. On this reading it is not Tyler who is the superman: it is Jack.

Appendices

Appendix A. Key quotes (DVD: approximate time code)

- 3.00: Jack's voice over (VO). Top floor of skyscraper with Tyler.
  'And suddenly I realise that all of this, the gun, the bombs, the revolution, has got something to do with a girl called Marla Singer.'

- 3.57: Jack VO. Jack and his co-workers at their photocopying machines.
  'With insomnia nothing is real, everything is far away; everything is a copy of a copy of a copy.'

- 31.14: Tyler to Jack. Lou's Bar.
  'The things you own end up owning you.'

- 39.28: Tyler in the bath at Paper Street. Jack sitting in the bathroom talking about their absentee or estranged fathers.
  Jack: *'I can't get married. I'm a 30 year-old boy.'*
  Tyler: *'We're a generation of men raised by women. I'm wondering if another woman is really the answer we need.'*

- 57.15: Jack to Cop on phone who thinks the explosion in Jack's apartment was deliberate.
  'That condo was my life ... that was not just a bunch of stuff that got destroyed ... it was me.'

- 1.10.11: Tyler imparts his philosophy to the guys of fight club.
  'Advertising has us chasing cars and clothes, working jobs we hate, so we can buy shit we don't need. We're the middle children of history, man: no purpose or place. We have no great war, no great depression. Our great war is a spiritual war; our great depression is our lives. We've all been raised on television to believe that one day we'll be millionaires and movie gods and rock stars. But we won't. We've slowly learnt that fact and we're very, very pissed off.'

- 1.24.28: Tyler delivers a monologue to the camera, which becomes so intense that the actual film jumps in the projection gate.
  'You're not your job. You're not how much money you have in the bank ... not the car you drive, not the contents of your wallet, not your fucking khakis.'

- 1.57.00: Jack meets Marla in an attempt to protect her from Tyler.
  Marla: *'You are Dr Jeckyll and Mr Jackass!'*
  Jack: *'I've come to realise I really like you Marla ... I care about you.'*

- 2.10.15: Tyler to Jack. The top floor of the Parker Morris building from the start of the film.
  'Out of these windows we will view the collapse of financial history. One step nearer to economic equilibrium.'

- 2.15.54: Tyler to Marla as they hold hands and the buildings before them are detonated and collapse.
  'You met me at a very strange time in my life.'

Appendix B. Further USA Contexts

Fight Club is very much an American product in terms of its cultural reference points even though it can clearly be read on generational rather than geographical lines. There are then some obscure (to UK audiences) references to 'Ozzie and Harriet' and 'Martha Stewart', for example, which need explanation.

'We were like Ozzie and Harriet.' (Jack VO)

This is an ironic (some might say homo-erotic) reference made by Jack to his relationship with Tyler in their Soap Street House. It is a nod to the longest-running US live-action sit-com *The Adventures of Ozzie and Harriet*, which ran on ABC from 1952 to 1966, and starred the real-life Nelson family. This straight-laced vision of 1950s failed to strike a nerve with the baby-boomers, who saw the show as a conventional repackaging of stereotypical gender identities and an anthem to suburban life.

'You know man, it could be worse; a woman could cut off your penis while you were sleeping and toss it out the window of a moving car.' (Tyler to Jack)

This is a reference to an infamous incident that really occurred in 1993 when John Wayne Bobbitt's wife, Lorena, cut off his penis with a kitchen knife and threw it from the window of her car. The incident became notorious, largely due to the fact that the penis was found and reattached to Bobbitt. The operation was so successful that Bobbitt went on to feature in porn films. Tyler's comment adds fuel to the notion that *Fight Club* is obsessed with male-castration fantasies, locating male power in the genitals and exhibiting a terror of emancipated women.

'I say, fuck Martha Stewart.' (Tyler to Jack)

This refers to the US media personality, food and furnishings guru Martha Stewart who runs her own media company, Martha Stewart Omnimedia. Her website lists her output as follows (I include it verbatim as it reads as a catalogue of all the things Jack and Tyler hate):

Martha's creative vision is the blueprint for *Martha Stewart Living Omnimedia* and the expansive multimedia and merchandising portfolio that includes award-winning magazines such as *Martha Stewart Living* and *Martha Stewart Weddings*; the nationally syndicated, Emmy Award-winning television series *The Martha Stewart Show*; *Martha Stewart Living Radio* on Sirius XM; the *marthastewart.com* website; best-selling books like *Martha Stewart's Cooking School* and *Martha Stewart's Homekeeping Handbook*; the *Martha Stewart Collection* of products for the home at Macy's; *Martha Stewart Everyday* mass-market merchandise at Kmart; *Martha Stewart Crafts* with EK Success; *Martha Stewart Furniture* with Bernhardt; *Martha Stewart-designed homes* and communities with KB Home; *Martha Stewart Rugs* with Safavieh; and more. (marthastewart.com. July 2011)

Appendix C. Recommended Viewing

Feature films directed by David Fincher

Alien 3 (1992)
Seven (1995)
The Game (1997)
Fight Club (1999)
Panic Room (2002)
Zodiac (2007)
The Curious Case of Benjamin Button (2008)
The Social Network (2010)
The Girl with the Dragon Tattoo (2011)

Selected advertisements directed by David Fincher

American Cancer Society – Smoking Foetus (1984)
Nike – Instant Karma (1992)
Coca Cola – Zero City Blade Rollers (1994)
AT&T – 'You Will' campaign (1995)
Levi – The Chase (1996)
Adidas – Mechanical Legs (2002)
Heineken – Brad Pitt: Beer Run (2005)
Nike – Trail of Destruction (2009)

Selected music videos directed by David Fincher

Aerosmith – *Janie's Got a Gun* (1989)
Madonna – *Express Yourself* (1989)
Madonna – *Vogue* (1990)
Rolling Stones – *Love is Strong* (1994)

Selected feature films starring Edward Norton

Primal Fear (1996)
Everyone Says I Love You (1996)
American History X (1998)

25th Hour (2002)
The Illusionist (2006)
The Incredible Hulk (2008)

Selected feature films starring Brad Pitt

Thelma & Louise (1991)
Interview with the Vampire (1994)
Twelve Monkeys (1995)
Snatch (2000)
Troy (2004)
The Assassination of Jesse James by the Coward Robert Ford (2007)
Burn after Reading (2008)
Inglourious Basterds (2009)
The Tree of Life (2011)

Selected feature films starring Helena Bonham Carter

Lady Jane (1986)
Howard's End (1992)
Planet of the Apes (2001)
Sweeney Todd (2007)
The King's Speech (2010)
Alice in Wonderland (2010)
Harry Potter series (2007, 2009, 2010, 2011)

Other key films of 1999

American Beauty (1999)
Being John Malkovich (1999)
Magnolia (1999)
The Matrix (1999)

Other films of influence and analogy

Rebel without a Cause (1955)

The Graduate (1967)
Butch Cassidy and the Sundance Kid (1969)
A Clockwork Orange (1971)
American Graffiti (1973)
Alien (1979)
Natural Born Killers (1994)
Trainspotting (1996)
American Psycho (2000)
Bowling for Columbine (2002)
Choke (2008)
Capitalism: a love story (2009)

Bibliography

Abu-Jaber, D. (24 November 1999) Susan Faludi coaches *Fight Club* author *Salon.com* (online) Available at http://www.salon.com/1999/11/24/faludi_4/ [Accessed 4 December 2011]

Bentley-Baker, D. (August 2010) What is Cult Cinema? *Bright Lights* [online]. Issue 69. Available at http://www.brightlightsfilm.com/69/69cult_bentleybaker.php [Accessed 16 November 2011]

Benyahia, S. C., Gaffney, F., White, J. (eds) (2009) *A2 Film Studies: The Essential Introduction* (2nd edn.) UK: Routledge

Beradinelli, J. (1999) *reelviews.net* (online) Available at http://www.reelviews.net/movies/f/fight_club.html [Accessed 4 December 2011]

Biography channel.co.uk Available at http://www.thebiographychannel.co.uk/biographies/brad-pitt.html [Accessed 4 December 2011]

Bly, R. *Iron John: A book about Men* (1990) Addison-Wesley

Box Office Mojo *Top Box Office Hits of 1999* Available at http://boxofficemojo.com/yearly/chart/?view2=worldwide&yr=1999&p=.htm [Accessed 4 December 2011]

Bradshaw, P. (12 November 1999) *The Guardian.* Available at http://film.guardian.co.uk/News_Story/Critic_Review/Guardian_review/0,4267,102483,00.html [Accessed on 4 December 2011]

Browning, M. (2010) *David Fincher – Films That Scar.* USA: Praeger

Chandler and Tallon (2008) Poverty and Anarchy in *Fight Club* in *You do not talk about Fight Club*, edited by Read, Mercer, Scuchdart. Benbella Books

Crampton, R. (27 November 2010). *The Sunday Times Magazine* (cover story) 'Why are Men so Unhappy?'

Cultographie's Defintion of Cult Cinema (Editorial) *Cultographies.com* [Accessed: 3 December 2011] Available at: http://www.cultographies.com/definition.shtml

The Cult. The official Chuck Palahniuk Web Site. Available at: http://chuckpalahniuk.net [Accessed 3 December 2011]

Ebert, R. (15 October 1999) *The Chicago-Sun Times* Available at http://

rogerebert.suntimes.com/apps/pbcs.dll/article?AID=/19991015/
REVIEWS/910150302 [Accessed on 4 December 2011]

Edward Norton Discusses *Fight Club*: *Yale university* (October 1999)
Available at http://edward-norton.org/articles/yaleint.html [Accessed 3
December 2011]

Faludi, S. (1999). *Stiffed: The Betrayal of the American Man*. William
Morrow and Company inc.

Fight Club DVD (2006). DVD booklet. Fox

Fight Club BluRay (2009). Fox

Giroux, H. (2001) *Private satisfactions and public disorder: Fight Club,
patriarchy and the politics of masculine violence*. Available at http://www.
henryagiroux.com/online_articles/fight_club.htm [Accessed 4 December
2011]

Gordinier, J. (26 November 1999) 1999: The Year that changed
Movies. *Entertainment Weekly* Available at http://www.ew.com/ew/
article/0,,271806,00.html [Accessed 4 December 2011]

IMDb – *Internet Movie Database* Available at: http://www.imdb.com/
[Accessed: 3 December 2011]

Jane Austen's Fight Club.com Available at: http://janeaustensfightclub.
com/ [Accessed 3 December 2011]

Kaczynski, T. (1995) *Industrial Society and its Future*. Available at http://
editions-hache.com/essais/pdf/kaczynski2.pdf [Accessed 4 December
2011]

Kavadlo, J. (2008) The fiction of self-destruction in *You do not talk about
Fight Club*, edited by Read, Mercer, Schuchdart. Benbella Books

Keegan, R. (3 May 2007) The Time 100 – 1997. *Time*. Available
at: http://www.time.com/time/specials/2007/time100/
article/0,28804,1595326_1595332_1616809,00.html [Accessed 4 December
2011]

Lim, D. (6 November 2011) '*Fight Club*' Fight Goes On. *The New York
Times* [online]. Available at: http://www.nytimes.com/2009/11/08/movies/
homevideo/08lim.html [Accessed: 3 December 2011]

Mantz, S. (1999) *moviemantz.com* Available at http://www.moviemantz.
com/movie_reviews/1099/fight_club.html [Accessed 4 December 2011]

Maslin, J. (15 October 1999) *Fight Club*: Such a very long way from duvets
to danger. *The New York Times* Available at http://movies.nytimes.com/
movie/review?res=9506E1DE1030F936A25753C1A96F958260 [Accessed on
4 December 2011]

Maslin, J. *12 Monkeys*: A Time Traveller with Bad News *The New York
Times*. (27 December 1995). Available at: http://movies.nytimes.com/
movie/review?res=9D03E7DF1239F934A15751C1A963958260&partner=Rott
en%20Tomatoes [Accessed: 4 December 2011]

Mechanic, B. (September 2009) *Film mogul's bad decisions* Available at:
http://www.raindance.org/site/index.php?id=46,4902,0,0,1,0&highlight=me
chanic [Accessed: 3 December 2011]

Morrow, L. (19 August 1991) The child is the father of the man: Robert
Bly *Time Magazine*. Available at http://www.time.com/time/magazine/
article/0,9171,973647,00.html [Accessed 4 December 2011]

Halpern, S. (September/October 1999 Issue) *Susan Faludi: The Mother
Jones interview*. Available at http://motherjones.com/media/1999/09/
susan-faludi-mother-jones-interview [Accessed 4 December 2011]

News Corp. Available at: ://www.newscorp.com/operations/index.html.
[Accessed: 3 December 2011]

Nietzsche, F (1885) *Thus Spoke Zarathustra* Cambridge University Press
2006

Nietzsche, F (1886) *Beyond Good and Evil* Penguin 2003

Nietzsche, F (1887) *On the Genealogy of Morality* Hackett Publishing 1998

Nietzsche, F (1888) *Twilight of the Idols* Cambridge University Press 2006

Nietzsche, F (1888) *Ecce Homo* Cambridge university Press 2006

Palahniuk C. (1996) *Fight Club* Vintage (2006 UK edition)

Phillips, G. (12 August 2010). The legend of *Expendables* body count: just how
many people have they killed? *Heyuguys.co.uk* [online] Available at: http://
www.heyuguys.co.uk/2010/08/12/the-legends-of-expendables-body-count-
just-how-many-people-have-they-killed/ [Accessed: 3 December 2011]

PRNnewswire (1999). *Fight Club: A 'Thelma & Louise' for Today's Men Fighting a Gender War* Available at http://www.prnewswire.com/news-releases/newsweek-susan-faludi-on-fight-club--a-thelma--louise-for-todays-men-fighting-a-gender-war-76670222.html [Accessed 4 December 2011]

Rooney, D. (12 September 1999) *Fight Club* Review. *Variety*. Available at: http://www.variety.com/review/VE1117752116?refcatid=31 [Accessed: 4 December 2011]

Sbbfc (Students' British Board of Film Classification) Available at http://www.sbbfc.co.uk/CaseStudies/Fight_Club [Accessed 4 December 2011]

Schuchardt, R. M. (ed.) (2008) *You Do Not Talk About Fight Club*. USA: Benbella Books

Screenit.com Available at: http://www.screenit.com/ [Accessed on 4 December 2011]

Seitz, M, Z. (10 November 1994) Bloodlust. *The Dallas Observer*. Available at: http://www.dallasobserver.com/1994-11-10/film/bloodlust/ [Accessed: 4 December 2011]

SimplyBrad.Com Available at: http://simplybrad.com/brad-info/biography/ [Accessed : 4 December 2011]

Smith, A. (2009) *Empire Magazine* Available at http://www.empireonline.com/reviews/reviewcomplete.asp?FID=5168 [Accessed: 4 December 2011]

Smith. G, *Film Comment*, (September 1999) Volume 35, No 5

Stein, J (25 October 1999) The Emasculation Proclamation. *Time Magazine*. Available at http://www.time.com/time/magazine/article/0,9171,992347,00.html#ixzz1fkhX6bKC [Accessed 4 December 1999]

Stewart, M. *marthastewart.com* Available at http://www.marthastewart.com/

Suicidegirls.com (13 January 2011) *Fight Club photo-shoot* http://suicidegirls.com/albums/site/13576/gallery/html/ [Accessed 3 December 2011]

Swallow, J. (2004) *Dark Eye - The Films of David Fincher*. UK: Reynolds and Hearn

Taubin, A. (1999) So good it hurts. *Sight and Sound*. Available at http://www.bfi.org.uk/sightandsound/feature/193 [Accessed 4 December 2011]

UK Birth Statistics (June 2010) Available at: www.statistics.gov.uk [Accessed: 3 December 2011]

Vacker, B. (2008) Slugging Nothing in *You do not talk about Fight Club*, edited by Read, Mercer and Schuchdart. Benbella Books

Waxman, S. (2005) *Rebels on the Backlot* USA: HarperCollins.

Walker, A. *London Evening Standard* (11 November 1999) Available at: http://www.compsoc.man.ac.uk/~heather/mustard/walker.htm [Accessed on 4 December 2011]

Also available from Auteur

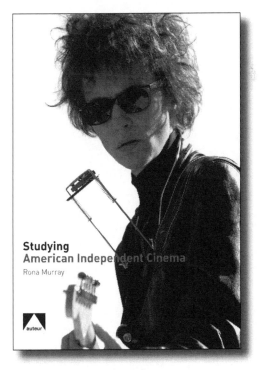

**Studying
American Independent Cinema**

Rona Murray

£17.99
978-1-906733-17-9

"This student-focused guide explores modern US independent cinema in depth and places it in context of its more general history. Starting with John Cassavetes and *Shadows*, it focuses on case studies of key films, blending detailed textual analysis with an exploration of each text's wider theoretical and historical contexts. Discussions of Miramax and the Sundance Film Festival are paired with case studies of the work of Steven Soderbergh (*sex, lies and videotape*), Quentin Tarantino (*Pulp Fiction*), Todd Haynes (*I'm Not There*), Gus Van Sant (*Last Days*), David Lynch (*Mulholland Drive*), John Sayles (*The Return of the Secaucus Seven*), Kimberly Peirce (*Boys Don't Cry*), Spike Lee (*Do the Right Thing*) and PT Anderson (*There Will Be Blood*). Rona Murray examines their diverse inspirations, such as European cinema aesthetics, previous independent film-makers and wider film history."

auteur